Mirjana Stanislava Vasilj-Zuccarini

Our Lady's Call from Medjugorje

® Copyright ®: Mirjana Stanislava Vasilj-Zuccarini
ISBN 88-8424-099-9
e-mail: mirjana@ime-screens.com

http://www.medjugorje.mi.it

Original title: "Gospin poziv iz Medjugorja"
Translated from Croatian: Nenad Vukasović

Corrections: Schwanhild Heintschel-Heinegg

Cover Design: Ing. Martina Vasilj

Photo by kind concession of:
© Informativni Centar "Mir", Medjugorje ©
© Father Gabriele Amorth, Rom (Italy) ©
© Pietro Jacopini, Fermo (Italy) ©
© Schwanhild Heintschel-Heinegg ©
© Prof. Ferdinand Graf ©
© Klaus Flörchinger ©
© "Gebetsaktion" Vienna (Austria) ©
© Mario Vasilj and Vinko Dragičević, Medjugorje ©

The photos of Father Slavko are published with exclusive
permission from Mrs. Schwanhild Heintschel-Heinegg,
Prof. Ferdinand Graf, Mr. Klaus Flörchinger and
"Gebetsaktion".

16th EDITION
The book has been translated into 21 languages.

To my parents Jelena and Ante, my cousins and all the parishioners of Medjugorje, and also the friars and sisters who, strengthened by thousands of years of devotion to the Blessed Virgin Mary, bravely and resolutely built an insurmountable "wall" of prayers and fasting around the six visionaries. Many were the insults. Brutal ones too! But, thanks to the entire parish community, which immediately adopted Our Lady's messages, these apparitions have seen world wide echo and have not vanished, as has happened all too often, in the recent history of the Church.

Many thanks to Norma Bullen, Joan Madden, Felicity Ashton, Donatella Giannini Cassanmagnago, Elisabetta Codara, Alison Trezzi and Nenad Vukasović, who have helped with the creation of this book in English language!

"*Our Lady's call from Medjugorje*" *is no makeshift book but a text which has developed over many years in the mind and heart of the author Mirjana Vasilj Zuccarini, who lives in Merate, Italy.*

The book, for those who are familiar with the happenings of Medjugorje, is a pleasant journey through the memory of long years of apparitions. The author's search, neither easy nor short, will certainly spur the reader to a meeting with Medjugorje ... either repeated ... or for the first time ... so as to hear its strong heartbeat for today's man.

Prof. Krešimir Šego
Editor "Mir" Medjugorje

The writer is from Medjugorje where, for many long years, mysterious events have taken place, making headlines all over the world.

Mirjana has retained, in mind and mood, a strong attachment to her birthplace and people and antique ideals of faith. She has lived the story of the apparitions with intimate and keen participation because she knows the visionaries and the people of Medjugorje personally.

From this experience, which is animated by a spirit of investigation, she has written an enthralling and truthful work.

Prof. Gildo Spaziante
Author of "Studies of Medjugorje"

Another book on Medjugorje! Who on earth needs it? To be quite honest ... I do...! Hoping that you, dear readers, could use it too, so that you can get a clearer picture of the events. I also hope that this book might inspire you to understand the messages from Our Lady more easily and to identify yourselves with them.

In the beginning, back in 1981, when Our Lady was reported to have visited six visionaries for the first time, there was an atmosphere of distrust, fear and anxiety. Therefore it was not possible to gather and preserve all the visionaries' testimonies at one place and without disturbance. Nowadays, after a quarter of a century, many documents have emerged and I have used these to describe the events chronologically. Furthermore, I have included my memories presenting them in first person.

Where is Medjugorje in the first place? Who are its inhabitants? What are they like? I do know many of them personally, as it is my ancestors' homeland; therefore, before assuming the role of chronicler, I will use various sources, from the past and present, in order to introduce the reader to the Medjugorje parish and its parishioners.

The more I progressed with my work the clearer it became to me that there was no coincidence and that Medjugorje's geographical position is an ideal location for sending an urgent worldwide appeal for peace.

A small Catholic parish, unknown to the world, heavily oppressed by the totalitarian atheistic regime, was chosen to accept a heavenly invitation for reconciliation with its age-old history and neighbours of other religions having the same roots. Let us not forget, Medjugorje is located in the Federation of Bosnia and Hercegovina inhabited by Catholics, Muslims and Orthodox Christians.

It is only now, many years after the first apparition, that we dare say that heaven has come to earth to eradicate religious, racial and class prejudices imposed by those who hold mundane power and who oppose the saving power of Christ.

Besides, the Blessed Virgin has come to warn us of the dangers of dissolute materialism that leads us directly to practical atheism. Day by day, over many long years, Our Lady has been inviting us, has been inviting me, but you as well, all of us, to join the universal redemption action in saving mankind, as Mother of all the peoples announced in Fatima back in 1917.

The Church does not oblige us to believe in any of the Marian apparitions; but in spite of this it is good to know that Pope John Paul II kept a vigilant eye on events in Medjugorje and personally appreciated them.

I have distanced myself from any interpretation of the Medjugorje events and I have assumed the role of pure chronicler of the apparitions of Our Lady because, if they were originated by the Almighty, and I believe they were, they are well beyond the reach of any limited human mind. It is difficult to describe God's acts in words. Words can only inspire the reader to come to the source of grace by himself and to feel, in his heart, how much God loves him and how much He cares for him.

The Author

MEDJUGORJE:
People and History

The parish of Medjugorje is situated in the western part of Hercegovina south of Mostar on the 43rd parallel - just like Assisi. It includes five small villages: Medjugorje, Bijakovići, Vionica, Miletina and Šurmanci. It is in the Čitluk district, in the historic Brotnjo area. The village is named after its geographical location - among the hills.

It is populated by the Croats, an ancient people, whose name, according to established Russian and German historians, has its roots in pre-Christian civilizations around the Persian Gulf. These opinions are supported by the archaic words: "hor-va(t)" (path of the Sun) and "hu-urvata" (friend). Within living memory, Croats have had a red and white checkerboard as their coat of arms, but very few actually know if it symbolizes opposite forces in the battle of life or not.

In the late Bronze Age the Illyrians inhabited the Medjugorje area. During the first centuries of the Christian Era, Roman veterans made their home there. It is very probable that the Croats settled in Brotnjo in the seventh century. There are several theories about their arrival in the Balkans. The theory that attracted my attention most was the one claiming that the Croats, according to the Emperor of Byzantine, the historian Constantine Porfirogenet's writings, had escaped the Huns from the east and reached today's Kharkow where they established their state: White Croatia. Ancient Croats named the corners of the earth by colours and the colour white meant west. Far away from their original eastern home and surrounded by Slavic nations, Croats adopted their own language and customs and their own polytheistic faith. The same historian also states that Istanbul was endangered by the Huns, ferocious barbarians, in the early seventh century and the Byzantine emperor Heraclius appealed to the Croats for help. He even mentions seven brothers who brought Croatian tribes to the Balkans.

The Croats won and seized power, dominated the Christians, Illyrians and Romans and enslaved them. Therefore Pope John IV (640-642) sent abbot Martin, laiden with gold, to pay the ransom for the Christians and bring the relics of Istrian

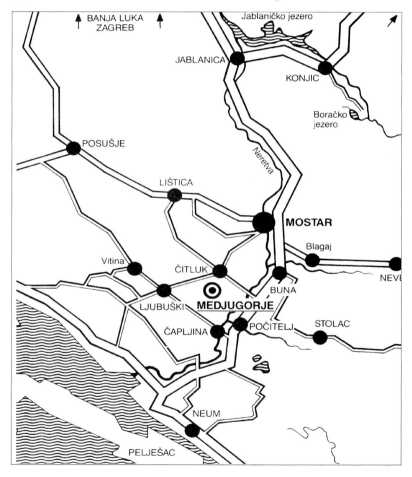

and Dalmatian martyrs to Rome. The abbot discovered that the Croats were ready to bargain which enabled him to complete his mission successfully. Shortly after, the Pope sent priests to convert the Croats to Christianity. According to this story, it would seem that a drop or more of the blood of ancient Christians from the Balkans, Romans and Illyrians, runs in the veins of the inhabitants of Medjugorje.

After adopting Christianity, the Croats swore to Saint Peter Apostle never to conquer other countries and to live in peace with the neighbouring nations that were willing to do so too, retaining the right to defend themselves in the name of Christ, should anyone attack them. Faith in the Catholic Church and loyalty to the Pope, St. Peter's successor, is one of the major distinctions of the Medjugorje inhabitants, almost as if they themselves had sworn to Peter's Successor in Rome thirteen centuries ago.

During the expansion of Christianity in the Balkans, in 1054 there was a schism that split the Church into the Roman Catholic and the Orthodox Eastern Church. One hundred years later, the influence of the schism was visible in the Trebinje diocese, east of Medjugorje, when it was conquered by the Serbian rulers the Nemanjićs who officially began to convert "Latin heretics", as they called them, to the Eastern Orthodox religion. The historian priest Dukljan and the monk Theodosius reported this. The Orthodox Church obliged people to be re-baptized, while the Catholic Church upheld the validity of both baptisms. Such a practice continued during the entire Middle Ages, when it was quite usual for a sovereign to decide on his people's religion: "Cuius regio, eius religio!" (Whose kingdom, his religion). No wonder that under the rule of Emperor Dušan the "Powerful" Catholics were forced to convert to the Eastern Orthodox Church and that the Emperor's subjects continued to sell Croatian priests as slaves and burn down their churches in order to exterminate any trace of their culture.

The Croats who in the 12th century did not have a king or a powerful state, defended their faith with all their might. They prayed, fasted and made a vow to Our Lady, asking Her to ask God to protect them. They went on pilgrimages to Rome to ask for help from the Pope. Even the great Italian poet Dante writes "... devoted as Croatian pilgrims".

Remnants of the troubled Middle Ages in Medjugorje and surrounding areas can be seen in tombstones, the so-called "stećci"; human-shaped crosses with arms raised in prayer are sculptured into many of them. The human nature of the authors is attested by inscriptions that may be found on some crosses: "Please do not step on me: I was like you are once, you will be like I am some day" or "I have been lying here long since and I have to continue doing so for quite a while yet".

Franciscan Missionaries

The Catholic Church was weakened in the Balkans in the Middle Ages not only because of the expansion of the Orthodox Eastern Church, but also due to the presence of various sects, like the Patarens and the Bogomils present in Bosnia at the time. Therefore the Vatican first sent the Dominican monks and then the Franciscans, who, shortly after their arrival, expanded their pastoral work from the Black Sea to Istria and from the Adriatic to Budapest. There are numerous church remnants witnessing their fruitful work.

The period of expansion of the Christian culture was rudely interrupted by the Turkish conquest which enslaved

Bosnia in 1463 and Hercegovina in 1482. The Franciscan friars were exterminated or were forced to hide and share all poverty and want with the common people. They were priests, doctors and teachers. Being united this way, they managed to preserve Catholicism. It was, however, extremely difficult, as most of the people escaped from Hercegovina to unsettled parts of Dalmatia which was under Venetian, Catholic domination.

Not all Croats resisted Islam. Many of them, in order to preserve their property, conformed to it. This is how the Muslims emerged, being no longer identified with the people they had descended from. Pope Leo X encouraged the Croats' to resist and used to call them "bulwarks of Christianity". They paid dearly for such a position: thousands were killed during the war against the Turks and they lost the central part of the territory they once inhabited: Bosnia and Hercegovina.

The Turkish reign of terror lasted for more than four centuries before it came to an end in 1878, when Bosnia and Hercegovina first came under the authority of the Austrian-Hungarian Empire and was annexed shortly thereafter. Croats from Hercegovina were even separated from the mother country in Austria-Hungary. As for religion, under these new conditions they enjoyed great liberty: churches were built, new orders were established, Catholic schools were opened.

The Franciscan province of the Assumption was established in Mostar in 1892. In the very same year, the Parish of Medjugorje was founded. The first thing the monks did was to build a church. Unfortunately they chose inferior terrain: it was a terrain that had been said to be unsuitable by an old dowser who said there was a great cave underneath and predicted that the soil would cave in. Indeed this happened thirty years later: the walls of the church cracked, the church tower leaned so the church became unstable and for years the masseses were celebrated in the open air, in the church yard in summer, while in winter they went to the parish house basement.

The inhabitants of Medjugorje enjoyed religious freedom for only twenty years. The Great War started in 1914. My ancestors, of Vasilj-Grgasović descent, lived in a five-family community: men were fighting wars while their children were starving at home. Likewise, many other children were starving so Father Didak Buntić moved about twelve thousand children from Hercegovina to Slavonija (in the north of Croatia) and saved them from death. This tragedy was followed by the epidemic of the Spanish Flu, which killed many inhabitants, my grandmother Stojka among them, leaving her husband, four daughters and a ten-year old son Ante, my father.

After the Great War ended and the Austrian-Hungarian Empire fell apart, under the protection of the allies led by Great Britain, the Kingdom of Serbs, Croats and Slovenians was created. Alexander, an Eastern Orthodox Serb, related to the English royal house, was crowned king.

During the first Yugoslavia, the Orthodox Church put strong pressure on the Catholic clergy to renounce the Holy Seat and celibacy, forcing them to use Cyrillic scripts and to wear beards so that they looked like Greek Orthodox priests. Belgrade witnessed successful mass demonstrations, against the signing of the Concordat which the Vatican endeavoured to arange with the Kingdom of Yugoslavia in order to protect the Catholics.

Croatian Catholics, those from Hercegovina, were certainly not willing to renounce their national identity and a faith that they had preserved for centuries at great sacrifice. Proud, rebellious and quick-tempered, they would not submit. They repelled attacks by sticking together. They suffered famine more than any other people, because famine was, at that time of great worldwide economic crisis, the major peril for the people.

The most important agricultural product in Medjugorje and most parts of Hercegovina was tobacco, a state monopoly that was so poorly paid that peasants did not earn enough to pay the taxes. People had to sell goods on the black market but inspections were severe and the police watched not only the roads, but forest paths as well. My father Ante and his uncle Nikola had a small wine shop at the time and they frequently used to go north to sell. Their fellow peasants gave them their tobacco to transport to Slavonija and exchange it for flour.

The Votive Cross

A Parish Priest, Father Bernardin Smoljan, who experienced famine and poverty, endeavouring to unite his exhausted parishioners, made a vow to build a great cross on Šipovac hill in memory of the 1900th anniversary of Jesus' passion and death. In doing so, he aimed to dedicate his parish to Christ, the Saviour of the world and thus protect it from any evil, including hail which often destroyed the vineyards and tobacco plantations.

The parishioners agreed and, some were barefoot as, on foot, they carried bags of cement, iron bars, wooden beams and other things that my father had transported to the foot of the hill which was 537 meters high. Since then the Šipovac Hill has been called Križevac. A ten-meter cross was made by masters Ante-Redžo Dugandžić from Miletina and Nikola Vasilj-Grlić. Holy relics - parts of the Crucifix of Christ, expecially brought from Rome, were placed at the intersection of the cross. The entire parish went uphill towards the cross on the day of consecration, walking rocky ground and thornbushes, where sage and ash-wood grew. They said their rosaries and sang the Virgin's Plea. The Parish Priest blessed the cross and Father Grgo Vasilj, born in Medjugorje, celebrated the first Holy Mass. Since then, every year in September Holy Mass has been celebrated on Križevac.

The faithful of Medjugorje did not leave the cross to safeguard the village alone, but from the very beginning there were numerous quiet pilgrimages. Whenever one was worried, he would go there. People used to go to the cross on their bare knees, over sharp stones. On the Eve of Midsummer Day 1937, Father Jenko Vasilj, murdered several years later during the war, celebrated the Virgin's Mass.

*The Votive Cross
(33-1933)*

On that occasion parishioners illuminated the cross and made a chalice of kerosene lamp flames with a host above. People who came from the surrounding places watched the scene with joy.

Father Bernard Smoljan wanted to build a new, larger church but as he lacked funds he could do little other than lay the foundations. The architect Stjepan Podhorski from Zagreb made church designs that were changed by Father Pijo Nuić several years later he reduced the naves. Just before World War II, the building of quite a large church for such a small village had started. Tradition has it that the architect said that he had designed a church that one day would be too small.

World War II arrived, more horrific than the Great War, transformed into civil war in the ex-kingdom of Yugoslavia. The antagonism between Croats and Serbs reached its peak. The Croats longed for independence, as they could no longer stand eight centuries of slavery under foreign oppression. On the other hand, the Serbs did not want to lose their privileges or the dominant role they had exercised over other nations in the Balkans and they endeavoured to strengthen their own power.

In a time of general confusion, the communist commander Tito, supported by partisans, reached the river Isonzo in Italy. Churchill, the English Prime Minister at the time, asked the allies if they intended to let Tito conquer Rome. It was this politician, who supported Tito and enabled him to establish the New Yugoslavia from the ashes of the old one. It was a Babylon of six republics, where there were three official languages and three different religions: Roman Catholic, Greek Orthodox and Islam. This happened under an atheist communist regime, a dangerous enemy of the faith, which did its utmost to separate man's soul from God.

While the war was reaching an end, Croatian Catholics, as well as many others, were withdrawing from communism to Austria. The allies, who were supposed to protect armies and civilians that surrendered, sent them back to Yugoslav partisans. Two hundred thousand died during this Way of the Cross. Partisans executed summarily, in flight, especially Croats from Hercegovina. My maternal grandmother Andja and grandfather Mate miraculously survived this Calvary and when they got back, with their three younger children, to their home near Medjugorje, which had been totally stripped and robbed, grandmother saw the crucifix on the bedroom wall and said, full of hope and faith: "The enemies took everything from us but God's blessing!"

Hundreds of priests were executed in Bosnia and Hercegovina immediately after the war. The Parish Priest, directly responsible for the great votive cross of Medjugorje, was killed in Mostar along with Father Grgo Vasilj. Both of them were thrown into the Neretva river, so their grave is unknown. The entire Church property was confiscated and the clergy was pauperized.

Medjugorje lost 368 inhabitants in the War. Many others fled abroad. My mother, not knowing if her husband was dead or alive, took my little brother and me away, walking for days, without food, towards Zagreb. After great suffering my family gathered and settled down in the town of Opatija in Croatia.

After the War, the Communist Party immediately showed its true face, by repealing catechism in schools. At the time I completed the first class of elementary junior school, and I was taught in catechism lessons that God had created the world. In the second class I was taught that there was no God and that man descended from apes.

The new social order, which was a deed of the Antichrist, was supposedly based on the freedom of the common working man who was guaranteed to live in brotherhood and harmony, but at the price of relentless criticism and persecution of those who used their heads.

The hidden but real objective was to raise generations of obedient dependents, who would always live in fear and mutual distrust as this way they were more easily controlled.

The Difficult Life of Those who Believed

The new authority immediately started to teach children the history that suited it best. Again, the Croats were obliged to keep silent about their history and learn about other history. This was especially so with regard to the most recent historical facts, referring to the War that had just ended, where a one-track approach prevailed. From childhood children were taught to hate Germans, Italians and home traitors who were responsible for horrible crimes that innocent people suffered during the war. Naturally, the struggle of absolutely "innocent" partisans and popular heroes, was glorified. The clergy was besmirched in order to drive people from the Church.

While in the Socialist Federal Republic of Yugoslavia seeds of hate and intolerance were sown, in Germany, which had lost the war, children were taught about the harmful effects of nationalism that had brought the people to ruin. The "Diary of Anna Frank" was compulsory reading, which helped young Germans to see the disaster caused by the arrogance and desire to establish a Great Germany. In Italy, the post-war Christian

Democratic government kept silent about fascism and their alliance with the Germans and thus missed a remarkable chance to objectively present mistakes of the past and distance themselves from them. This was later cleverly used by the extreme left wing politicians. They condemned everything related to fascism and won over a considerable part of the nation imperceptibly encouraging them to gradually renounce their strong religious principles.

The Archbishop of Split, Frane Franić, now retired, told me about oppression exercised by communism for years after the war aiming to divide the Catholic Church prelates from the Vatican and to establish the Croatian National Church analogically to the Serbian Orthodox Church. Once, while he was speaking on the Italian Radio Maria, he explained how they had forbidden him and his priests to use public intercity transportation for pastoral visits to their parishes. They told them: "You are fascist, go on foot!" And, so they did, all over their diocese! He also told of how he avoided imprisonment because he had been chaplain in Split prison and had helped those communists, who were harassed by the Old Yugoslav authorities at the time. Now that they were in power they protected him. This example shows that, regardless of any circumstance, one must always show compassion and understanding for those who suffer.

Like the clergy who did not bow to pressure, the people did not either, and they avoided employment in civil services and careers in the communist party, because they knew that they would have to renounce their religion, therefore few Croats were highly ranked. The same can be said for the Muslims who were not great in number as they respected their religion, too. The Orthodox Church cooperated with the communists and their faith weakened, they allowed their churches to be closed and the people not to be baptized. As such, the Serbian people, who were in the majority, became good servants to the new atheistic regime and therefore gained leading positions. They achieved wealth but they lost touch with their religious roots.

The coexistence of the Catholics and Orthodox in post-war Yugoslavia was not easy, although there were mixed marriages. However, such marriages, where children were raised in no particular religion, were rare in western Hercegovina, as local Catholics were devoted to Jesus Christ, Our Lady and their religion. Communists endeavoured to break such a firm faith and they persecuted, tortured and jailed people from the diocese of Mostar-Duvno, which Medjugorje belongs to. More than seventeen thousand people were killed in this diocese after the war.

Also my father, although far away from Hercegovina, was not exempt from psychical torture. Once a week he had to meet the party secretary who expected him to report what the priest had talked about in his sermon during Sunday service. My father's answer was always the same, that the church was open and that nobody hindered him from going and listening himself. They broke neither him nor us, and we used to go to the half empty church in Opatija to attend Holy Mass.

The communists were systematically pushing Hercegovina into the background, in terms of economy so that in the early sixties Croats were forced to look for jobs in Germany, Austria, Sweden, Australia and America. One day, while I was in my first year in college in Zagreb, I saw quite a long queue in front of the German consulate. There were men who had been waiting for a work permit for as long as three days; there were many men from Medjugorje. They went to work in Germany as labourers and they lived in poor shacks.

The government fostered and induced such an exodus hoping that, in this way, it would get rid of this invincible and proud people. On the other hand the inhabitants of Medjugorje did not intend to stay abroad forever: they left their wives and numerous children at home to work the land but they were sure they would be back soon.

In dificult moments of temptation, their wives addressed themselves to Jesus and Mary: they often went up Križevac hill, barefoot and with a rosary in their hands. They went in silence, discreetly. They went up the hill strong in the belief that Christ could destroy all arrows of the evil one and save them and their families by virtue of the cross. They recited trienas and novenas, fasted on Friday in honor of Jesus, sometimes on Tuesday, to ask for help from St. Anthony. Women and old men sought protection from friars, who were themselves oppressed, and entrusted them with all their sufferings and hardships of life without their husbands or sons.

Old Marićiuša, the shepherdess, talked about Our Lady saying She would appear in the thorn-bush valley and that a strange future would come and bring a white army to Medjugorje. Everybody laughed at her stories and no one took her seriously, neither the elderly nor the young ... especially the young!

From ancient times the usual greeting in Medjugorje was "Praised be to Jesus and Mary!" In the early sixties the young people, influenced by popular Italian songs, used to say "ciao"! This displeased the elderly Fillip Pavlović from Bijakovići who used to say to the young people: "Alas! Look at yourselves, woe to you when Our Lady comes, you'll crawl into a rat hole!"

My uncle Janko, a painter, wrote on his garden wall the following words in large letters: "DJIZU PRONAM!" (Praise be to Jesus) in an Asian language and used to say to the children: "What' does it mean ciao? You animals? Even in the Far East Christians greet each other with "Praise be to Jesus!'" and you have forgotten it!" The inscription was written in a strange language so that the communists could not understand it!

Janko often made jokes at the atheists' expense, either real or invented ones, they would wink at him because he was in poor health, so they thought he was absolutely harmless.

They did not realize his providence. This unconventional person, brought up in various big cities after the war, was aware of the many perils lurking for the younger generation; therefore he returned to Medjugorje as soon as he married because it was only there that he felt he would be able to raise his children in the real Christian spirit. He succeed in doing so with all of his five children.

The New Church

Years passed and the church, which was started immediately before the war, did not advance farther than the foundations. The inhabitants of Medjugorje persistently applied for a permit to continue the building but all their requests were refused until 1966.

As soon as the permit was obtained all the parishioners took part in the construction: some by working, some gave money. The most significant contribution was provided by those who worked abroad and those who emigrated.

This way the construction of a large church with two bell-towers was completed. From both sides of the main entrance there were ten windows pointing upwards: an invitation to contemplate twenty centuries of Christianity. The outer walls were painted in blue and yellow while the interior irradiated celestial brightness through three soft colors: pink, light blue and light yellow, painted like all churches following the tradition of the common people. Just like the old, ruined church, this one was dedicated to St. James, the patron of pilgrims, the intercessor between God and the people.

Even the choice of the Parish Patron was inspired by heaven. St. James Senior, the apostle martyr, abandoned everything in order to follow Christ. Strong and brave, he succeeded in converting the man who took him to the place where he was beheaded on king Herod's order. His ashes

Pilgrims found no seats in the church

were brought to Spain. For centuries pilgrims have visited his grave in Compostella. It was because of these pilgrimages that Spain succeeded in repelling Saracen Muslim attacks, thus remaining part of Christian Europe.

People from neighbouring villages came to see the great church of Medjugorje. One of them, finding himself in front of the church one Sunday, asked those present why there were two bell-towers. His attitude was of roguish criticism. My uncle Janko heard him and took him by surprise "What do you mean why? How many are there in Notre Dame in Paris?'

The consecration of this large church had been a kind of holy aim for the inhabitants of Medjugorje, who were descendants of those pagans who had become Christians there thirteen centuries before. They were now grateful to be able to thank God for all the help and love received in this beautiful temple, by singing: "We praise thee, Oh God" with all their hearts.

Vlado Falak from Šurmanci, a naive painter, had made a painting showing Our Lady soaring between heaven and above Križevac beneath, while the new church was in the left corner of the picture. What inspired him, although absolutely unconsciously, to foresee future events? The painting was exhibited in the church choir for a long time.

Overjoyed with the church, the inhabitants of Medjugorje made solemn preparations for the celebration on Križevac. They even managed to obtain an electric cable which was more than a thousand meters long and connected it to Ante Dugandžić's house thus supplying electricity to all the Stations of the cross and to the cross itself. For the nine nights before the celebration of the cross, Križevac was shining in the night as if it had been a mystical vision coming from heaven to earth. Passengers who travelled from Mostar to Ljubuški, halted on the main road to enjoy this unusual and beautiful scene.

Life was hard in every village of the Medjugorje area, even in the late seventies. They planted tobacco and grapes with their backs bent, drove cattle on rocky ground. At noon, when the bells rang, they halted with their hoes in their hands and said loudly: "Praise be God and St. James". They crossed themselves: "In the name of the Father, the Son and the Holy Spirit!" Then they devoutly hailed Our Lady: "Angel of the Lord...." They prayed the "Lord's Prayer" and "Hail Mary" for the dead who had earned and left them what they now had. After the prayer, they had their meagre lunch and returned to work.

Towards evening, they drove sheep into the pen and the sheep pushed each other with their bells ringing. In the early morning the cocks crowed and woke up sleepy peasants for another new day. This was summertime.

The children play with a small donkey

Sometimes, in winter, while the young joked light-heartedly and laughed together, the elderly gathered around whispering among themselves of the injustice they suffered and lamenting their need for freedom and peace.

The inhabitants of Medjugorje, like millions of others, were overwhelmed by the problems of mere survival. They did not have time to think of the history of suffering ... that it was a miniature reflection of the general suffering of the human race, for which every human being assumes his own responsibility when, misled by satan, he silences his conscience and allows the weeds of envy, jealousy, hate and greed grow within.

Throughout history, such weaknesses of people has often been used, and still are used, by some secular and religious leaders all over the world. Leaders who speak so beautifully about peace, justice and freedom secretly, cause wars, revolutions, commotions in order to gain worldwide glory, honour, power and wealth. By doing so they abuse the free will that God has given to all of us. But we people are often at fault as our weaknesses and mistakes provide the rich soil necessary for planting with dragoon seeds of hate, intolerance, violence and revenge.

In 1980, twenty years before the end of the last century, the inhabitants of Medjugorje could not possibly have dreamt that Our Lady would suddenly appear among them and call them to convert themselves; that She would require them to pray and fast - these being the only means that would provide them with their longed desired freedom and drive away any peril, even the danger of a war that was lay an ambush, of which they were totally unaware.

Not even in their wildest imagination could they foresee that our Lady would visit them, making their hearts thrill, as they heard Her sweet words: "Dear children, I have chosen your parish for a special reason."

Could they ever have guessed that their small village would be flooded by incessant streams of pilgrims from all over the world? That statesmen, princes, prelates, people of other religions, diplomats, writers, scientists, common believers and hundreds of the sick seeking consolation and hope for their sufferings and pains would swarm to visit their parish and church?

They could not possibly have thought that millions of pilgrims would visit their small village ... and that these pilgrims would leave with faces lit-up with happiness. Ready to witness, in a hundred different languages, of how they had found God, through prayer, in Medjugorje. Of the peace in their souls which was beyond any power of description, such peace that, being firm in their conversion, would bring the desired peace on earth.

How could they know?

OUR LADY
at Medjugorje

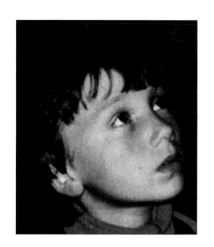

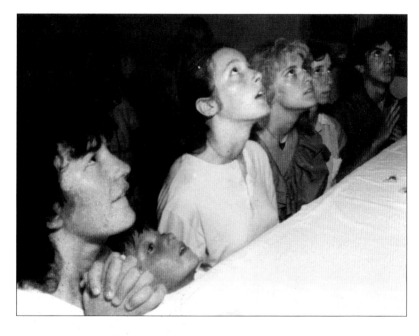

Father Jozo Zovko

In mid November 1980 the Parish Priest Father Luka Sušac, an old fashioned friar, left the parish of Medjugorje where four hundred families then lived. He was replaced by another Franciscan, forty-year old Father Jozo Zovko, who had come from the big parish of Posušje northwest of Hercegovina.

A modest and straightforward man, a priest of strong faith, contemplative and charismatic, Zovko strongly influenced the young people. Gentle by nature, but firm in his attitudes, he used to say that he was sorry, but that he had no intention of wedding or baptizing anyone secretly; those who came to church furtively to save their careers. He was a thorn in the flesh for the communists as they believed that he was responsible for the fact that the youth of Posušje did not join the Communist Party, so they, the Communist Party, asked the Church to transfer him to some other parish as soon as possible.

The small village of Medjugorje was chosen. After the war more than forty friars and sisters had taken their vows there so, according to the authorities nothing worse than that could happen!

The day after his arrival at his new parish where nobody knew him, Iva Šego (who lived in one of the furthest houses under Križevac), went on foot, to attend Mass. She used to go every morning, regardless of the weather, saying her rosary on the way from her house to the church. She felt sorry that Father Luka had left because she had gotten to know him well and she was a little troubled as she was going to meet the new Parish Priest who was completely unknown to her. As soon as Iva reached the church she saw Father Jozo walking slowly, step by step, along the nave towards the sacristy. She thought: 'He walks calmly, nicely, he does not rush, he looks capable and sincere, it will be easy with him'.

The new priest gave no idea to anyone of his inner suffering at having to leave Posušje so soon after having set up so many projects there. He overcame his sorrow and he devoted himself to his parishioners with all his heart. Here, too, he organized prayer groups for the young people, introduced them to meditation and taught them spontaneous prayers. He was an excellent catechist and he taught the doctrines with great enthusiasm and expected much of his pupils. The Church allowed the eating of meat on Friday and some members of the Franciscan order had slipped into this habit. He advise them to obstain again, as they used to, to the glory and honor of Jesus.

Father Jozo endeavoured to involve the parish and to help them appreciate Holy Communion more deeply. He wanted to help them feel Christ's presence and encouraged them to stay a few minutes longer in the church after Mass ended. His experience told him that it would be more difficult with men and therefore he asked them to leave the church at the end of Holy Mass while the women remained. They would sit in silence and follow his instructions for the meditation which was something unknown to them:

"Let your back be straight, close your eyes gently, relax as much as you can, and while you inhale and exhale calmly, repeat quietly to yourselves: Jes-us, Jes-us, Jes-us. Tell Him everything that troubles you, He will help you and understand your pain because He loves you immensely!"

My aunt Anica, who was hard of hearing, did not hear what the priest had said and when she saw her daughter sitting still, with her eyes closed, she exclaimed loudly:

"Zdenka, you have fallen asleep, get up, let's go home!"

The women took to meditation immediately because it enabled them to see how close Jesus was and because these moments of rest for the soul and body were a real blessing.

Father Jozo was very different from his predecessor, even while offering Mass: his mass was much longer and he made long pauses during his sermons. Some older parishioners were bored and used to say that his sermons and Masses were too lengthy, they compared Jozo with Father Radovan who celebrated a Mass in half an hour, and Father Luka in forty-five minutes, while he Jozo was neverending so he should be substituted as soon as possible! When they asked old Pavo, who babbled and twanged, what he thought about the new priest, he said:

"Tso, Tso, he seems nice, but I can't figure out what he wants with his pauses and silences in the middle of the sermon".

The Feast of John the Baptist

On Wednesday, June 24th, 1981, Midsummer Day, Father Jozo was conducting spiritual exercises for the Franciscans Sister in Kloštar Ivanić near Zagreb. They prayed together for his new parish which was exposed to various dangers. The friar attempted, as he had previously done for several days, to telephone his chaplain, Father Zrinko Čuvalo who had remained in Medjugorje. He did not know that lightning had struck and set fire to the community home where the post office was along with a newly-opened disco for young people.

From the early morning the heat had been unbearable in Medjugorje.

Two girls: fifteen year old Ivanka Ivanković and sixteen year old Mirjana Dragičević from Bijakovići, a village near Medjugorje, went for a walk in that hot afternoon, heading as usual, towards Perkuša, a place outside the village at the bottom of the Mount Crnica. Ivanka mourned for her mother who had died less than two months before. Her father was working in Germany and she was visiting her grandmother with her elder brother and younger sister. She attended Grammar School in Mostar. She could be described as a good-natured modern, sweet-tempered, straightforward and balanced person.

Mirjana the other girl came from Sarajevo to visit her grandmother in Bijakovići for the summer vacations. She lived in Sarajevo with her mother Milena, a worker, her father Jozo, radiographer and a younger brother. There she attended second grade at Grammar School. She could be said to be quiet but firm, reserved and also sweet natured - a normal girl, who did not show off because she lived in the capital of Bosnia and Hercegovina.

The two friends were chattring together as they took the path leading away from the village walking up the slope of Mount Crnica. On their way back, Ivanka instinctively turned her head to the right and looking upwards, towards a place called Podbrdo Hill saw the figure of a young woman flooded by intense light. Astonished, she yelled:

"Look, Our Lady!"

"Oh yes...Our Lady! Come on!"

Mirjana interrupted her immediately and, without stopping to stare upwards she carried on her way. Stumbling, as if in a trance, Ivanka followed her, her heart throbbing.

Before they entered the village they met thirteen-year-old Milka Pavlović, who being happy to see them said:

"Come with me to get the sheep."

They went with her. Ivanka could not keep quiet any more and she begged her friends to return to the same place to see if the young woman was still standing there. The other two girls looked at each other, hesitating, then they agreed to follow her, just to convince her that she had not seen anything.

The moment Mirjana and Milka reached the bottom of the hill and looked upwards about a hundred meters they too saw the Madonna. Mirjana noticed that the woman was wearing a dress that was not of these times. She had a child in Her arms. Ivanka was absolutely sure that it was Our Lady.

While they were standing there, as if frozen, contemplating the heavenly vision, Ivanka's cousin, seventeen-year-old

Ivanka

Mirjana

Vida Ivanković, called Vicka, awoke from an afternoon nap. On that sultry, hot morning she had gone to Mostar to sit for a mathematics exam. Vicka, the fourth of eight children, lived in Bijakovići with her mother Zlata and her other brothers and sisters. Their Father Pero was away in Germany, working.

Everybody liked Vicka because she was joyful, straightforward, amiable and, above all, generous. On that day, as soon as she had woken-up, she had gone to meet her friends at the usual place outside of the village. From the distance she saw all three of them staring at the same point and she thought that they had seen a viper. As she reached them, Mirjana pointed her finger upwards and said:

"Look, Our Lady!"

Vicka did not look. Sandals in hand, she rushed away towards the village, where she sat on a rock, panting and sweating, arms around folded legs, she burst out crying. Vicka was so upset she did not know what to do; all she could do was cry. How could her friends joke about Our Lady?

She still had not calmed down when two boys came along: twenty year old Ivan Ivanković and sixteen year old Ivan Dragičević. Ivan was attending first grade at High School, he was shy and withdrawn and was the eldest child of farmers Zlata and Stanko. He had a bag full of apples in his hand and he offered one to Vicka.

She shook her head, wiped her tears away with her hand and repeated what her friends had told her they had seen on the hill and begged them to follow her:

"Come up there with me. Mirjana says that Our Lady is on Pobrdo hill. It's not that I don't want to see the Madonna but I'm afraid to go alone."

The two Ivans went back with Vicka and, when they reached Mirjana, Ivanka and Milka, they too saw the mysterious woman. The young Ivan, frightened by what he saw, threw his bag of apples away and ran in fright towards the village as fast as he could! The older Ivan said that he saw a figure in white that was moving.

Vicka clearly saw a beautiful, graceful girl. She noticed Her silvery-gray dress, Her shiny black curls falling under Her white veil. Her eyes were sky-blue. Eyelashes black as coal, mouth small, red, symmetrical, heart-shaped; cheeks rosy. Around Her head she saw a crown of twelve stars that were not tied or supported by anything. The mysterious Lady had a child in Her arms, covering and uncovering it with Her veil. Her feet were covered by a long dress. She stood on a soft cloud that hovered above the ground. Mirjana too saw the beautiful young Lady with the child in Her arms.

The beautiful creature waved to them to come closer, they looked at each other and whispered in fear: "She calls us, but who dares to go closer?!" The girls whispered they were afraid but their hearts were fluttering with joy and happiness.

The girls did not dare go any closer the magical place, they just watched until She disappeared. Their hearts were dancing with great pleasure, delight and happiness.

Vicka

Ivan

Vicka and Milka returned to the village before the others and ran into Milka's house. They found only fifteen-year old Marija, Milka's elder sister, who was attending the first grade of a hair stylist school. Their mother Iva also lived there. Their eldest sister was married and father Filip and their three brothers were in Germany where they worked.

Marija was a very shy, quiet cautious girl. She looked in astonishment as Milka and Vicka burst into the house, panting, and gasping excitedly while they told her that they had seen Our Lady on Podbrdo Hill. Marija's heart immediately started pounding, she was so excited that she could not say a word. To hide her excitement, she fixed her eyes upon the floor, but her face, lit up with a warm, mysterious smile, revealed that in her soul she already believed what she had heard.

Although she was usually withdrawn, Mirjana surprised herself, she could not keep what she had experienced to herself. She entered the neighbor's house where two girls were watching TV and told them that she had seen Our Lady up there on the hill a few minutes ago. The two girls jumped off the couch, turned off the TV, and one of them, little Jela, ran to her mother to tell her the news. She burst into her house and shouted: "Mummy, Mummy..." Her mother, who was saying the rosary with the younger brothers, put her finger on her lips, ordering her to be quiet. Jela sat by them and joined in the prayer. When she had finished the prayer, she told her mother that Our Lady had appeared on Podbrdo Hill. She believed her at once.

As soon as Mirjana entered her aunt's home she told her what she had seen up on the hill. Her aunt looked at her in silence and immediately telephoned her sister Milena in Sarajevo: "Praised be Jesus, sister, I have to tell you something, but I do not know how to go about it. Your Mirjana says that she has seen Our Lady on Podbrdo Hill!"

Mirjana's mother, although alarmed, asked her sister a sensible question:

"What's your impression, how is Mirjana? Like she always is, or is she not quite in her right mind?"

"She appears to be perfectly normal."

"Then she must have told the truth, she would never dare play games with Gospa (Our Lady)!" was her reply after the first shock and surprise.

The parents and most of the relatives of Vicka, Ivanka and Milka, tried to calm down the visionaries and bring them to their senses. Together they all repeated:

"Sshh! You mustn't say things like that. Respect Our Lady. Off you go to confession, at once!"

There were those who laughed at them and mocked them: "Who knows what you saw on the hill! An UFO or a ghost? You should have caught it!

Will She Come again?

Early in the morning of the next day, as if nothing had happened, Ivanka, Mirjana and Vicka went to pick tobacco in the fields. On their way back home, feeling sweaty and tired, they met some boys who shouted as they were passing:

"Here comes Our Lady!"

They paid no attention to what the boys were saying nor did they answer back. In silence and deep in thought, they asked themselves if they would see the same thing they had seen the day before when they went to the Podbrdo Hill that evening.

Vicka's mother, Zlata, did not want to go to the hill, she was very worried. She asked Marinko Ivanković and neighbors to accompany the children asking them:

"Please go and see what it's all about. I don't want anything bad to happen. What can I do alone with so many children?"

Marinko, who worked as mechanic in Čitluk, lived with his parents, his wife and three children in Bijakovići. He gladly agreed to escort the visionaries because he immediately realised that it was good thing if an older person were around to protect them if necessary, because four of the children's fathers were away from Medjugorje working in Germany, at the time.

Milka wanted to go to the hill too, but her mother thought that she was too young and wanted to protect her from any harm, so she told her to finish a job at home. If anyone has to go she thought, let it be Marija, elder daughter. She will be better able to judge what is going on. Marija, however, did not want to go at first with Vicka, Mirjana and Ivanka so she made up an excuse: "I can't go now" she said, "but if you see Her, call me!" Vicka promised to call her if they saw Our Lady up there again.

At about 6 o'clock, Ivanka, Mirjana and Vicka set off towards the slopes of Podbrdo Hill. Marinko with Šito and several women and children went along with them. Ivan Dragičević, who had ran away the night before, joined them, too. The older Ivan, did not want to go. According to him it was "just a collective hallucination or a childish prank".

It was almost 6.30. Ivanka was walking in front as the small party headed for the Podbrdo Hill. Mirjana and Vicka followed chattering. Suddenly, at the same time as the day before, Ivanka turned and said: "Look Our Lady!"

The three girls saw Her, and so did Ivan and an adult, a woman, who realised that the Madonna was beckoning them to go near Her. She exclaimed: "Run to Her. Can't you see She is beckoning you!"

Vicka turned back and rushed to the village to call Marija. She found Marija with her ten-year-old cousin Jakov Čolo, who was there by chance, because he did not normally associate with older children. He was a bright lively boy, the only son of Jake and Ante, who worked in Sarajevo. He lived with his mother and was enjoying his school holidays after successfully completing the fourth grade of Junior School.

Both, Marija and Jakov looked at Vicka with astonishment:

"Come, come, follow me!" she shouted panting from her hasty run down the hill.

"Where are we going?" was their puzzled reply.

"Up there, hurry up, Our Lady is there! She's waiting for us! Hurry up!"

Marija picked up her sandals from the entrance of the house and ran after Vicka and with Jakov uphill. Half way there, Vicka told them that Our Lady was way up on high. They did not see anything and Marija wanted to climb higher to join Ivanka, Mirjana and Ivan. When they arrived, Vicka saw Our Lady waving to them beckoning to come closer. Mirjana, Ivanka and Ivan saw this too and ran uphill, Vicka went after them followed by Marija and Jakov, who had not yet seen anything.

All those left behind were astonished to see how swiftly the children rushed uphill, running straight ahead seemingly to fly over the thorn-bushes and rocks, slippery with moss as if an invisible hand carried them from the bottom of the hill to where the Madonna was waiting.

An intensive triple flash of light lit up the sky. Everybody saw it just as the children prostrated themselves in front of Our

Lady together with little Jakov who shouted at the top of his voice: "I see Our Lady!"

Then Marija saw Her too! Marija was staring up and fell on her knees next to Jakov. Both of them were overwhelmed with fear but, instead of running away, they felt the desire to get closer to this heavenly apparition and meet Her. That day the Virgin Mary appeared, without the child. All six of them started to pray in unison:

"Our Father who art in heaven, hallowed be Thy name....."

Our Lady gently looked at each of them, seeming to caress each one with Her eyes, joining in the "Lord's Prayer" but listening silently during the "Hail Mary" then She joined them again for the "Glory be to the Father"....

After the prayer, Ivanka was the first who dared to ask Our Lady:

"Kako moja mama?" (How is my mother?)

"Dobro je majka, dobro je." (Mother is well, she is well.)

Marija

Jakov

They asked Her if She would come again. She nodded, confirming, and then disappeared.

Ivanka's brother, who was there too, thinking they had all gone crazy. He had seen them keps focusing on one point and moving their lips, but he neither heard nor saw anything. The children did not answer.

Their faces were lit with joy and it was clear that they were contemplating as if in a dream, the divine apparitions that filled their hearts with immense love. After the apparitions they realized that Jakov, had thrown himself on his knees on a thorn bush, but had no scratches and Marija who had knelt on a wasps' nest, had not been stung even once.

Little Jakov was smiling blissfully and said:

"How pretty She was. I have never seen such a beautiful woman. I would not care if I died now that I have seen Our Lady!"

In his childish innocence, Jakov was sure he had seen Our Lady because She had immediately attracted him and let him feel Her immense maternal love, so that he, as soon as he had seen Her, wished to stay with Her forever.

While going back downhill, the children saw Our Lady once more. She smiled and said:

"Goodbye, my angels!"

A woman asked all the visionaries if they were sure that they had seen Our Lady. Vicka replied:

"I am positive, I am more than sure!"

The children described Our Lady as a beautiful young woman. Her beauty could not be described in words. Her soft voice, touched your heart. They tried to describe Our Lady's blue eyes, but they had never seen such a shade of blue on earth.

Ivanka was crying as she walked. Once at home, she fell into her grandmother's arms, weeping. She was very excited because of the news about her mother as she missed her mother very much but she was sorry she could not share this magic moment with her mother.

Her father Ivan was in Germany and he heard all about the visions his daughter received of Our Lady. He was very afraid because he thought she was the only one. He calmed down however, when he learned that five other children had also had the visions. He supposed that this would only last a few days and then everything would blow over his little girl would be left in peace!

The word that Our Lady had comforted Ivanka and told her that her late mother was well, spread around the village. Everyone knew that Jagoda had been a pius woman and good mother but no one considered her a saint and therefore the news relieved the anxiety of death and gave everyone a new kind of hope.

Vicka took it in her stride, and although she was surprised like the others, she kept her feet on the ground and accepted this unexpected gift from heaven with her all heart. What worried her the most was how she should behave when she met Our Lady next time so she asked her grandmother how she should pray the next day while waiting for the apparition on the hill. Her grandmother advised her to pray exactly the same way they had always prayed in Medjugorje, especially during the winter months: the Creed and seven times the Lord's Prayer, Hail Mary and Glory Be, as a tribute to the Seven Dolours of Our Lady.

Her grandmother and the other elderly women told her to take holy water with her and sprinkle the apparition: "If it is Our Lady" they explained " She will stay and if it is a devil it will disappear without a trace as soon as it feels the water!" It had not occured to Vicka that it could have been a devil appearing, but she decided to follow their advice. It was an old custom in Medjugorje, once a week, for the mistress of the house to sprinkle every room of the house... the yard and the cowshed with holy water in order to remove any evil presence from the house.

When Mirjana went to bed that night, after the second appearance of Our Lady, she kept thinking of the indescribable harmony and beauty of Our Lady's face. She wanted to be able to contemplate it for ever. She did her best to remember every detail because she felt that it was too long to wait till tomorrow when she would see Our Lady again. She wondered why she, of all people, had received such wonderful grace ... she who was just an ordinary girl like hundreds of others? While she was thinking this, she felt the need to speak to Our Lady using her own words so she prayed:

"My Lady, teach me how to pray devotedly and show me how I can be useful and do good!"

Ivan withdrew even more into himself. He wondered how he, of all people, had been chosen to see Our Lady. He, who was no better than any of the others, neither as a young man nor as a christian. He kept asking himself why me? The picture was engraved in his heart while he secretly hoped that he would see the heavenly image again the next day and the day after and the day after that... forever.

Returning home, little Jakov burst into his house and yelled from the doorway:

"Mum, mum, I've seen Our Lady!"

"Oh yes, of course son" was his mother's amused reply.

"Really, mum, I swear to you ... I've seen Our Lady!"

"All right, son... You've seen the Holy Mother ... well ... we'll see about that!" Little Jakov's mother was worried.

"Mum, listen to me. Our Lady will return tomorrow!"

"Be quiet. You scare me!" She stood still staring at nothing.

Jakov was about to speak when the Holy Mother appeared, She was smiling at him reassuring him that She would find a way to calm down his troubled mother and give her the strength to sustain and support him. His mother did not see the vision. When the boy went to bed a little later he couldn't get to sleep. He asked himself: "Did I really see Our Lady?" His heart was thrilled because he still had the sweet inner vision of the Heavenly Mother smiling at him. To convince himself that everything he had experienced that day was true, he whispered: "Good night, Our Lady. You will come to see me again tomorrow, won't you?"

Vicka's cousin, Marinko Ivanković, went to inform the chaplain, Father Zrinko of what had happened on Podbrdo Hill. Father Zrinko was phlegmatic in character and the people loved him because of his great sense of humour, he calmly commented: "To whom it is granted to see, let him see ... to whom it is not, let him not see!"

The Feast of the Sacred Heart of Jesus

The village bus passed by in the early morning to pick up the inhabitants who needed to go to Čitluk on business. The driver told them all about how some children from Bijakovići had seen the Virgin Mary and how all those who went to Podbrdo Hill could see Her. His story agitated the families of Čilićs, Šegas, Ostojićs, Smoljans, Dugandžićs and others too in Medjugorje, such as Miletina, Vionica, Šurmanci and Čitluk.

Few people had telephones at the time. However, in spite of this the news travelled as far as Mostar and Ljubuški, so that on the third day following the second apparition, on 26th June, a great many people arrived at Medjugorje and set off for Podbrdo Hill.

Vicka, Mirjana, Ivanka, Ivan, Marija and Jakov were in great suspense all day long, and they kept asking what time it was. Time passed slowly. They feared that perhaps they had done something inappropriate and that this beautiful woman might not show herself any more. About five o'clock in the afternoon all six went towards the hill. Milka also accompanied them hoping that she too would see Our Lady again. She saw nothing more than the others who were there: a great triple flash of lightning which connected the sky to the earth. Despite the sunshine, the lightning was clearly visible in its rare and unusual brightness. The visionaries gave a sigh of relief!

The triple lightning was a sign that the Virgin would come at the same time as the two previous days!

There She was again ... much higher than the two previous days! As if driven by some mysterious force, the visionaries seemed to fly towards Her. Ivan and Jakov first, followed by the girls. They all fell on their knees in front of a huge rock surrounded by thornbushes and started to recite the Creed and the Lord's Prayer, Hail Mary, Glory to the Father, seven times each. They recited in one voice exactly as Vicka's grandmother had advised them.

The heat was unbearable, people jostled, pushing their own children among the visionaries. They trampled on Our Lady's long mantle and She disappeared. Not everyone had come out of devotion, some out of curiosity while others cursed and stepped on the feet of the kneeling visionaires, almost crushing them. Ivanka, Mirjana and Vicka fainted. Their friends and relatives managed to reach them and create a space around them so that they could regain to consciousness.

Our Lady reappeared when they started to pray again. Vicka took out the bottle of holy water and sprinkled all the water on the Holy Mother. While doing this she made the sign of the cross and said:

"In the name of the Father the Son and the Holy Spirit, if you are Our Lady, stay with us. If you are not, go away!"

Hearing this, Our Lady smiled graciously.

Mirjana felt encouraged and asked the mysterious Lady: "Please, tell us, who are you?"

"I am the Blessed Virgin Mary!" was the reply.

Jakov with his mother

Delighted with the answer, Mirjana asked about her grandfather who had died the year before. The Virgin Mary replied that he was well.

She begged Our Lady to leave them a sign for people to believe that they actually had seen Her in front of them as if She had been of flesh and blood. Our Lady promised nothing. Ivanka also asked if her mother, who had died alone in the hospital, had a message for her.

Our Lady reassured her with a nod: "Obey your grand-mother, be good and be kind to her because she is old and can not work any more."

"Our Lady, why did you choose us of all other children?"

"I do not always choose the best!"

Just before the apparition disappeared, Ivanka, encouraged by Marinko asked Our Lady why She had come amongst them and what She wanted. Our Lady took a long look at all the people, there each and every one, before She said:

"To keep you all united together because you are all true believers!"

The visionaries asked Our Lady if She would come again the next day and She nodded confirming this. According to Marinko, he calculated about three thousand people on the hill that evening. Together with friends and relatives he guarded the visionaries on their way back to the village from the curiosity and comments of some of the disappointed people who, having seen and heard nothing, hurled insults at the girls as they were passing by:

"Just look at her, Our Lady's girl! Look how trendily she dresses. She must be on drugs that's why she sees ghosts!"

After a while the Holy Mother appeared again to Her chosen few and said: "Go ... in God's Peace!"

Before the end of the slope Marija suddenly left the group and hurried to the left to a place called 'Lokvetina'. She fell down on her knees again for there she saw Our Lady once more, in front of her. Behind Our Lady was a huge dark cross; the Virgin's expression was sad as She said:

"Mir Mir Mir (Peace, peace, peace)! Let there be peace between God and man and let peace be restored...!"

Hearing these words, Marija was so terrified that she could not move. The other visionaries arrived and helped her to return home.

The Feast of the Immaculate Heart of Mary

On the fourth day of the apparitions, on Saturday morning 27th June, Father Jozo, on his way back from Zagreb, arrived at Mostar to visit his mother who was in hospital. He met Draga Ivanković, Marinko's wife, who was there owing to an injury she received in the factory where she worked. Her leg and arm were bandaged. He approached her and asked her what had happened to her but she shouted excitedly:

"Father Jozo, where is chaplain Father Zrinko? Our Lady appears to us, but he won't hear about it and we do not know where he is!"

She was shouting so much that the priest, at first, thought that something must have happened to the chaplain, but when she mentioned Our Lady he was completely confused. Perplexed, he asked: "What Lady?"

Without waiting for an answer he went his way convinced that the woman had hurt not only her leg and arm, but that she must have fallen and hit her head too!

On hearing about the apparitions, the members of the secret police, were convinced that the apparitions must be some kind of trick by the clerical-nationalists from Hercegovina because after Tito had died they wanted to separate from Yugoslavia.

So in the late morning the police went to Bijakovići with the intention of obliging all six visionaries to go to Čitluk to be examined by a doctor. When they got to the Pavlović's house they found Marija, Ivanka and Jakov sitting on a couch, resting after working in the fields. Mirjana and Vicka were sitting on the floor under the table, because it was cooler there. They were half-hidden by the table cloth when one of the policemen entered the room and asked for the children who had seen Our Lady. The two under the table could not help laughing at the thought that on seeing them underneath the table he would surely think them both mad. They all had to go to Čitluk. Only Jakov's mother managed to give her son a clean shirt as she did not want him to go wearing the dirty old one which was sticky with tobacco. The others went dressed as they were in their working clothes.

While the policemen were leading the children into the car to take them for questioning, their scared relatives warned them:

"Children be careful, don't accept anything to eat or drink, don't let them give you injections."

They took them to the clinic in Čitluk; Ivan was already there accompanied by his father who, rather than let his son go alone, was barefooted as he did not have time to put his shoes on before leaving. Ivan was the first to be given a very through medical examination. It was Vicka's turn next, she looked the doctor straight in the eyes and said:

"I'll come for an examination when I need it!" the doctor laughed and asked her to stretch out her arms.

"Here you are, two hands, five fingers on each of them, count!"

Then Mirjana and Ivanka entered. The doctor offered Mirjana a cigarette, which she refused politely saying that she did not smoke. He also told her to stretch out her arms which she did gladly to show him that her hands were not shaking and that she was not on drugs as they seemed to think!

While the other visionaries were being examined, the doctor received a phone-call ordering the children to Mostar to be seen by a psychiatrist there. The visionaries replied that they were not crazy and that they had no intention of finishing up in a mental home! They ran out of the medical surgery to find some way of getting home. Once on the street, as if in waiting, they met an acquaintance who immediately drove them to Medjugorje in his van.

While the children were still being examined in the clinic, Father Jozo arrived back in the parish. As soon as the nuns saw him, they said to him:

"Father Jozo, you've no idea what's been happening. Some children are saying that they see Our Lady on Podbrdo Hill. People are coming here from all over. The police have taken the children to Čitluk."

"What Lady? Who are these children?"

When he heard that there was also a certain Mirjana, who lived in Sarajevo and whom he did not know, he began to worry too. He asked the nuns where the people came from. The sister told him that some even came from Mostar and that many of them said that they had seen a light.

'Aha, they see a light?' thought Father Jozo beginning to suspect that perhaps the communist police had invented all of it in order to make him and his parish look ridiculous. It must be so, he thought, as there are no policemen around, either in uniform or in plain clothes so that obviously meant that they knew there was nothing to investigate!

In the early afternoon a great number of people was passing by the church on their way towards Podbrdo Hill. Many of them went into the church. So Father Jozo stood behind the altar and said resolutely:

"The Church is very rigid about apparitions. It investigates them carefully and fully until the truth is out! All we can and must do now ... is pray."

At the end of the prayers he asked them not to go to the hill. The people were disappointed with this Parish Priest who did not believe in the apparitions and he in turn was disappointed with the people who did not listen to him. Each and every one of them, set off for Podbrdo Hill as early as four o'clock in the afternoon in order not to be late for the apparition.

Father Jozo asked himself how people could be so naive wasting their time looking in other places for what they already had alive and present in the Communion: the Christ! What use were apparitions, be they real or not? He was rather worried that a great scandal would break out and discredit not only his parish but the Church as well and that the communists would triumph.

He decided to interrogate the children one by one and he was sure he would find out who had manipulated them. He ordered Father Zrinko to go to Bijakovići and bring them to him.

The very moment the Chaplain approached his car to go and fetch them, a van entered the churchyard. Inside were the five visionaries who had just arrived from Čitluk! Vicka jumped out and ran towards Father Jozo, her eyes brimming with joy:

"Father Jozo, where have you been till now....?"

The friar interrupted her and warned her that he was going to interrogate them all one by one.

He started with Jakov aiming to confuse him. Here is part of this conversation which was taped by Grgo Kozina a young parishioner from Medjugorje:

"Jakov, my boy, tell me all about your conversation with Our Lady."

"The first time She came, Our Lady did not say anything but "Go in God's peace", when we were leaving. That's all She said. The second day we asked: "Our Lady, why have you gathered us here". She said: "To keep you all united and because there are many true believers here."

"What else did She say?"

"She said that we were all to go in peace: She said to reconcile one with the other."

"And what did She look like when She arrived? Did you see Her coming down from the skies?"

"I did. Everything flashed three times when we saw Her. She suddenly appeared up there and we ran up there right away!"

"And when, for example, She left, did you still see Her while the others didn't?"

"Who? I don't know. I saw Her moving upwards and suddenly She vanished. When She speaks She sounds as if She's singing!"

"What do you mean She sounds as if She's singing? Can't She speak normally?"

"Of course She can speak normally! What I'm saying is that She speaks beautifully."

"Which language does She speak?"

"Ours, Croatian, like me."

"Did you see Our Lady with angels?"

"No, I did not see angels, just Our Lady!"

"Strange, Our Lady is always with angels!"

"I saw only Our Lady."

"Did you say anything about this to your mother'?"

"Yes I did.... Mom asked me, no rather she said: "Be quiet you scare me!""

"Aha, your mother is afraid. Do you pray together?"

People are waiting on Podbrdo, early at dawn

"We pray "Angel of the Lord" and other prayers every night and at the end we say: "Good night, Our Lady, look after me all night long!"

"Did anyone else see Our Lady, did Iva Šego see Her?"

"She did."

"Could I see Her?"

"Yes, you could!"

"I could see Her, how do you know that?"

"Well, it's like this... Iva goes to the church every day and she saw Her, so all you friars could see Her too."

"What would you do if somebody stopped you from going, if your mum told you not to go to see the apparitions?"

"I can't stop going, I want to go. I would say to her: "Mum I will go even if you kill me. You can kill me. I'll still go the same.""

"But God says that you must obey your mother. What do you say to that?"

"I'll go to God, up there, I'll go to Our Lady up there, and that's that."

"You will go tonight, won't you Jakov my boy? Tell me, what will you ask Her this evening? Did anybody suggest anything to you?"

"I will ask Her: "Our Lady, why have You come to us and what do You want to tell us?" - that's what I think I'll say. No one needs to tell me what to say! As if I don't know how to ask by myself."

The Priest Is still Suspicious

Deep in his heart, Father Jozo had to admit that little Jakov answered maturely and sincerely, but the priest was far from believing these stories and he was even more cautious when he started to interrogate Mirjana. Here is a part of their conversation:

"Tell me, where is your father and what does he do for a living?"

"In Sarajevo, he is a radiographer."

"Is he good? Does he go to church? Do you go to church?"

"Yes, both he and I go."

"Are there other boys and girls like you, for example, who pray?"

"Very few. I have a friend, she does not go to church regularly. She studies and she always makes excuses not to go."

"Do they harass you at school because you go to church?"

"Yes. You know how it is in Sarajevo. They mock me and say I'm behind the times. I'm different to the other five catholics in my class because I really believe in God and they don't."

"Tell me the truth, do you pray regularly, every night?"

"Yes. Every night."

"Are you reading any religious books?"

"Yes. I have the one about Lourdes. Somebody gave it me yesterday and I started to read it because I was eager to know what happened to that girl. A neighbour has taken the book to show it at work. To explain that these kind of apparitions have happened elswhere. I like reading the Bible too.."

"Describe your encounter with Our Lady."

"I saw Her on the hill, like this, (she shows), She had a child in Her arms and She covered it. She wore a veil on Her head, like this (she shows). Not that I got goose-pimpled from fear, but on the contrary a kind of pleasure flooded me. I was in a turmoil, really. I wanted to tell everyone what I saw and make them understand... I mean.... I was feeling happy, pleased, in a turmoil."

"Is She beautiful?"

"Wow! Fantastic/incredibly!"

"Have you ever seen a young lady like that before?"

"Never."

"How tall is She, is she smaller than you?"

"Like me. But She is very slender, ethereal,.... delicate, somehow."

"Did you pray during the apparition?"

"Well we did as soon as we reached the hill, we recited seven Our Fathers, seven Hail Mary's and seven Glory Bes, as our grandmothers had advised us. Then we started to ask questions of Our Lady. But, we couldn't continue because of all those people!"

"Would you prefer if nobody were there?"

"Oh, yes! They've promised us that everyone will be about twenty metres away tonight. You know it's so hot. They push ... They trample on our feet..."

"You are no longer a child, you are a grown girl, have you any particular wish that you would like Our Lady to fulfill?"

Leave us some sign ... anything, so that people will believe us. When we ask Her something, She does not reply, She just looks at the people and smiles!

"Did anyone in the crowd ask any questions?"

"Yes, when we returned yesterday. Our room was crowded with people, we think we've repeated everything at least a hundred times. Quite a lot of them believe us. It is not difficult for us to talk. Let the people hear."

After the conversation ended, the priest and the visionary Mirjana prayed together for some time.

That same afternoon a young man, Marko Soldo, set off with his family from Mostar to Bijakovići by car hoping that he would meet Mirjana whom he liked very much. On their way, they stopped in Čitluk and visited his aunt Mara who told them that Our Lady had appeared to six children from Bijakovići, Mirjana was among them. Marko believed the story immediately and thought that Mirjana had deserved it as she was a very good girl. He was sad as he thought that now it would be impossible to reach Mirjana and that she would surely become a nun. He was in the crowd that evening during the apparition but he did not see Mirjana, not even from a distance.

That fourth evening Marinko agreed with Father Zrinko to divide the visionaries. They wanted to test them. Marija and Jakov were to stay behind by the side of the road while Ivanka, Mirjana and Vicka were to go to the place where Our Lady had appeared the previous two days.

A woman, who wishes to remain anonymous, went to the hill for the first time that day. She did not believe that the Virgin Mary appeared there. She went because her eldest son had told her that these apparitions were real. Her son had said "D'you want to bet it's true? I'm going". So she decided to go too and see for herself. While she was climbing the hill she saw Marija, her face was red as she exclaimed: "She is here!"

Marija and Jakov rushed uphill instantly and she lost sight of them. At the same time she felt a kind of soft breeze and saw the hill above her become pink. In the middle, there was a light like the sun and inside the light was the luminous figure of the Mother. The vision struck her with happiness. Father Zrinko realized that there was something extraordinary about the manner in which the children rushed uphill away from them and he could see that they could not possibly catch up with them.

On that evening too there was a mass of people around the children. Everybody saw the intense light in the sky and many pushed towards the visionaries because they knew that Our Lady was with them.

There was a large bush in front of the children, a parishioner Kozina, who wanted to tape the conversation, wishing to get closer, stepped into the thorn-bushes. Vicka and Marija warned him to stop because he was treading on Our Lady's veil. Everytime somebody got too close, they would step on Her veil and Our Lady would disappear. Marinko, who had arrived in the meantime, managed to keep back the people from around the visionaries, and Our Lady appeared again.

The children told everybody to kneel. The people knelt, on rocks and thorn-bushes, wherever they found themselves. There were about fifteen thousand people on Podbrdo Hill that day. Who could ever know what was going on in the heart of all those people during the apparition? Perhaps no word can describe the deep inner experience within each and every person.

Those who were present that evening remember faces lit with happiness and tears of joy. They felt that the Blessed Virgin was among them, that they were loved, accepted by Her just the way they were, with all their virtues and imperfections. They suddenly felt absolutely free, loved by God and with open souls and hearts to each and every one around them. They were ready to give the love they received to their neighbours regardless of who they were or where they came from.

Unknown among the crowd, was a certain Zdravka from Mostar. She suffered from terrible headaches which made her faint. She also suffered from atrocious pains in another part of her body where she had had cancer surgery. During the prayer she suddenly felt warmth and a strong current all over her body. From that day onwards all her disorders and pains ceased, as she later witnessed in the parish house.

The parents of a small boy Ivan came to the hill seeking help. Their child had sores all over his body and suffered horrible pains so that he cried day and night. They picked the medicinal herbs on Podbrdo Hill, brought them home and washed Ivan in an infusion and, as they did so, the child recovered immediately. This event was recorded, too, in the Parish Chronicle.

The visionaries felt more self-confident with the Blessed Virgin Mary. By now they were more courageous and felt closer to the heavenly apparition. Mirjana explained to Our Lady how they had been accused of being drugged and epileptic and begged Her to help them. The Mother of God comforted her:

"My angels, there has always been injustice. Do not worry about it!"

After these words Our Lady disappeared while they continued to pray along with the crowd for some time more. While they were going downhill Our Lady appeared again. She bade them farewell:

"My angels, go in peace with God."

Ivan was not there on this occasion because his parents, afraid of the authorities, obliged him to stay at home. He intended to obey but, when the time for the apparition came, he could not stand it, he felt he must go so he ran out of the house and set off

The Vasilj: Father Stanko, Miljenko, Toše and Janko

for Podbrdo Hill He had only walked a few steps, when he got leg cramp. Ivan could not move. In that same moment he saw the Holy Mother in front of him, She was smiling gently at him, and She told him to be in peace. He returned home happily and told his mother that he had seen Our Lady again. She was deeply moved and she promised him she would not forbid him to go to Podbrdo Hill again.

Blessed Are Those who Believe

The following Sunday, after the Holy Mass, a woman angrily asked the Parish Priest:

"What are you doing to our children. Why do you encourage them? Don't you realize that the police will be after us because of this?"

He did not have time either to realize who the woman was, nor to explain that he agreed with her as she rushed towards Bijakovići without waiting for his answer.

Father Jozo shrugged his shoulders and thought that he also was not having an easy time seeing that the police were now harassing him more than ever. He too had plenty to complain about regarding the children. Within himself, he disapproved that so many curious people were running to the Podbrdo Hill rather than going to church. There were priests in plain clothes among them who had cameras instead of rosaries wishing to take pictures of the visionaries. By no means did he feel easy about everything and he was alert for any indication or sign which would help him discover where and how it had all started. Jozo wished to save his parish from any further trouble.

Unhappy and worried, he entered the parish house and found Ivanka waiting for him. As for the girl, the priest thought, she is so upset because of her mother's death she might possibly imagine she sees the Virgin. He remembered the recent funeral when he himself was deeply moved because of the young woman's death.

Reluctantly, he had to ask her some things too. Here is a part of their conversation:

"Ivanka, do you know that those people passing by the church are angry because they neither hear nor see anything. You know, they are disappointed, puzzled and upset."

"What can I do? It's not my fault!"

"Yes ... But those people think that the ones who see Our Lady should look different to you all. That's the problem."

"I.. tell you honestely, I sobbed my heart out, even the third time I saw Her. When we asked Her to leave us some sign, She was turning around, She just turned Her head, looked at the people and smiled."

"I know, but why doesn't She leave a sign?"

"Well, I do not know. She said that people must really believe."

"Is it hard for you that everybody questions you, even we priests? I'd like to know how you feel when you speak to people and you realize they don't believe you."

"Me? I am telling you that I did see Her, whether you believe it or not. But it will all be proved!"

"Tell me what you heard from Our Lady, not what the others heard."

"I heard Vicka asking Our Lady to leave a sign. Our Lady nodded like this (imitating Her) and She said: "People should believe completely as if they had seen me". We asked the same for the friars. She told us that they too should believe completely."

"Did you touch Our Lady?"

"I did, it was as if my fingers sort of glided when I touched Her.... fingers gliding somehow."

After Ivan, who responded briefly with yes or no and had confirmed what the other visionaries had confided to the friar, it was Vicka's turn. She kept her presence of mind in spite of the ambiguous questions and showed her determination to devote herself to Our Lady regardless of the distrust and police pressure that they had already experienced.

On the fifth day the visionaries retold their conversation with Our Lady to Grgo Kozina who taped it.

"Dear Lady, what do You want from us?"

"Faith and Your respect."

"Dear Lady, what do You want from our priests?"

"I want them to believe firmly and preserve the faith of their people."

"Dear Lady, why don't You appear in the Church so everybody can see you?"

"Blessed are those who do not see me but who believe."

"Dear Lady will You come again?"

She nodded, confirming.

"Dear Lady, what do You prefer us to do, to pray or sing?"

"Both."

"Dear Lady, what do You want from these people?"

"Dear Lady, will You leave a sign for these people to believe?"

"Go in God's peace."

Our Lady disappeared in the light that was around Her. The people sang "How beautiful You are, Virgin Mary!" Marinko had to protect the visionaries while they were going downhill. The people were aggressive and Marinko suggested that the children say that Our Lady would only appear for the next three days. The children also wished to be alone during the apparition and they were sorry to hear every kind of insult that the communist agents and others were hurling at them and, especially, at their parents. They were incredibly vulgar in insulting their mothers.

On the sixth day, Monday, 29th June, early in the morning, on the Feast of St. Peter and Paul, the police came to take the visionaries by force to Mostar Mental Hospital. Vicka's mother stood up against them and asked them if they had a warrant. They shouted rudely to her and told her to be careful as otherwise they would beat her up. The doctors, in agreement with the police, were to scare the children and force them to stop "gathering people". To achieve this, they used illegal means: they took them to the morgue, where there was an unbearable smell.

They took them to a lunatic, who yelled and walked around them and watched them blank-eyed as if he were lost. The children almost went out of their minds. Then they took them to psychiatrists for an examination, among them were police in disguise. One of the doctors shouted rudely at them as she saw them in the corridor:

"Don't think you're going to ruin our country after all the blood that's been spilt!"

During the examination, one of the commission asked little Jakov:

"Have you seen Our Lady?"

"I have."

"What would you do for Her?"

"I would die for Her!"

The doctor thought for a moment and then said that he had no further questions. He obviously realized that no child could answer in that adult manner, unless there was something mysterious and unfathomable which was obviously beyond the nature and the power of the boy.

While Mirjana was waiting to see the doctor, nurses and other staff gathered around her and asked her quietly to talk about the apparitions. While she was telling them her experiences she noticed that they were so touched that their eyes brimmed with tears.

After having examined all the visionaries, one of the members of the commission, psychiatrist Mulija Džudža, a Muslim, said: "I have never seen brighter children than these, the one who brought them here is insane."

The children immediately forgot the violence they had suffered that day and they looked forward with great joy to their sixth meeting with the Heavenly Being from the skies. That evening a man carried a little boy Danijel Šetka in his arms up there on Podbrdo Hill, close to the visionaries. The child was deaf and paralyzed. His head drooped on his father's shoulder. As soon as Our Lady appeared, the children begged Her:

"Dear Lady, can You make little Danijel well again? Make a miracle for everybody to see!"

Our Lady looked at the child with infinate tenderness and graciously said:

"Let the parents pray, they should believe totally firmly and they should fast. Go in God's peace."

"Ode ..."(She went away...), whispered the children.

The people heard what the visionaries had said and started singing to the glory of Our Lady. Witnesses say that little Danijel got well after a little while.

The Apparition at Cerno

The communist authorities could not understand what was happening in Medjugorje and they did not believe that people were going there without being invited. Mirjana, a social worker, spent all the morning on Tuesday, 30th June, at meetings of the Trade Unions, the police station and the town hall. They all asked her for support because she was the visionaries' neighbour. She arrived in Bijakovići, accompanied by her colleague Ljubica, Head of Police, Trade Union president and Executive Committee. When they arrived at Bijakovići, they went to the visionary Mirjana's house and told her to summon all the visionaries for questioning. The visionary did not accept this. In order to win her over, the social workers suggested organizing an excursion. The parents let the children go with them as they trusted them. The two women immediately took them in their car thus avoiding any encounter with the Head of Police.

Marija, Vicka, Ivanka, Mirjana and Jakov went on the excursion. They were taken to Čapljina. They were offered fruit juices to drink. Little Jakov asked if they had to pay for only the juice or the bottle as well. They saw a seesaw in a park and Jakov had to try it out. Vicka also sat on the seesaw and flew up and down. The little boy looked at her. He was fascinated and happy because it was the first time he had ever left Medjugorje and had never seen so many wonderful things before. Even the car ride was a great novelty for him, and as he said later, he had ridden to his heart's content.

About half past six the children asked Mirjana, the social worker, to stop the car, right there in Cerno, where they were at that moment. She pretended not to hear them, but soon she had to stop because a very bright light suddenly appeared almost blinding her. The visionaries got out of the car and walked away from the road. They knelt and faced Podbrdo Hill which could be seen in the distance, flooded by intense light. The light moved towards the children and with it Our Lady appeared. They began to pray and then suddenly became silent. The social workers watched them, their lips moving, but they could not hear what they were saying. They advised the children to ask Our Lady if She would appear in the church. Yes, tomorrow at the same time, the children replied. The two women asked for how many more days they would see Our Lady. They replied, as Marinko had advised them, by saying for three more days, childishly hoping that everybody would leave them alone.

The other social worker Ljubica saw the light going away from them and hang over the people waiting for the children in vain on Podbrdo Hill. An acquaintance of mine was among the people. She was six months pregnant. A woman behind her encouraged her saying: "Just go ahead, sister, don't be afraid, if you need something I am here, I am a midwife!" My acquaintance told me that people were quiet that day on the hill and that they prayed with great devotion.

The two social workers accompanied the children to the parish house and told the Parish Priest what they had experienced. The visionaries told Father Jozo that Our Lady would appear in the church. He replied that there was no time to inform the people before Sunday, and that the people would not go to church but directly to the hill. The visionaries told him not to worry for, the people would come without invitation.

The Apparitions in the Church

Early in the morning on the eighth day, Wednesday, 1st July, the visionaries' parents were called to the Primary School for interrogation. The secret police agents threatened their parents that they would declare the children insane, ban them from school if they did not oblige the children to stop the "circus".

The parents were not afraid and they defended their children bravely. Later on, around noon, the police took Vicka's mother, Zlata, to Čitluk and kept her there till early evening. (They threatened her harshly and told her that she and her family would experience great trouble if she refused to cooperate). They tried to make her forbid her daughter Vicka, whom they considered the leader, to go to church and ordered her to do her best and stop this "nonsense". Zlata replied:

"I'll see what I can do about it, but I really do not know how anyone can forbid the children from seeing the apparitions."

In the afternoon, two men from the local secret police arrived at Bijakovići, supposedly to offer a drink. Jakov's mother managed to hide him. Ivanka, Marija and Vicka got into their car accompanied by Vicka's sister and Ivanka's brother. The car was a station wagon and when they passed the church and the bridge, Our Lady suddenly appeared in the car with them. She smiled and told them not to worry. Marija and Ivanka were scared out of their wits because the policemen were present during the apparition. The police called them witches. Vicka, who was a little more sure of herself, told them to take them back. The other three visionaries saw the Holy Virgin by themselves in Bijakovići, near their homes.

That very same evening, at about six o'clock Father Jozo was quite surprised to see that people were spontaneously coming into the church. Some of them wanted to confess. Father Zrinko was saying the rosary and the Parish Priest talked about Christians who obtained strength from the sacraments and the Gospel. He mentioned Lourdes and Fatima as a very special heavenly invitation to men who had forgotten God. He emphasized that it was a tragedy that modern man had forgotten God and did not ask him for help in everyday life. Jozo realized that the people were listening to him more carefully than usual and he told them to pray, either in church or at home, for the grace of understanding if what was happening was an act of God or not.

After the apparition, the children confirmed that Our Lady had said that She wanted people to gather in the church to recite the "Creed" and repeat the "Lord's Prayer" and "Hail Mary" and "Glory Be" everyday seven times. Hearing this, the congregation fell on their knees and prayed.

On the ninth day, Thursday, 2nd July, the visionaries came to the church and recited the Lord's Prayer, Hail Mary and Glory Be seven times and the Creed, along with the congregation. Friar Jozo celebrated Holy Mass since it was the best he was able to offer to the pilgrims, who from mere passive observers were now active spectators in the apparitions of Our Lady. After the Mass Father Jozo told them:

The room of the apparitions, adjacent to the altar (1983)

"And now the girls will tell you about their experiences during the past few days and then you will hear a boy speak who is not even as tall as the altar."

Jakov showed himself to everyone and then started to speak:

"I asked Our Lady to leave us a sign and She nodded that She would. She said "Goodbye, my angels".

While the little boy was talking, everybody in the church was absolutely silent and then, as all of them were touched by his words, they started to sing "Sred te se pećine Marija javi!" (Our Lady appeared in the middle of the cave!). After singing and praying Father Jozo asked the people:

"Are you all willing to accept with love to do a three day fast, and eat anything for three days and thus withstand satanic temptations and drive away the evil that separates us all?"

"We are willing!"

"Are you willing to pray with your families, at home, everyday?"

Father Jozo celebrates the Eucharist

"We are willing!"

"Are you willing to read the Holy Bible in your family every day?"

"We are willing!"

The reply in unison was resolute and so convincing that Father Jozo realized that something remarkable was happening in the parish.

On the afternoon of the tenth day, Friday, 3rd July, the police returned to the visionaries' homes to take them away again. They did not find them as they sneaked over the tobacco fields and vineyards to the church.

In the meantime, Father Jozo was alone in church reading the Bible. He felt that it was time to clear his position with the people regarding the events of the past ten days. He prayed like this:

"O, Lord, You spoke to Abraham, Moses and many others. Hundreds of thousands are arriving here: Tell me, which path I should take, help me to understand what is happening here, let me know the truth!"

As he was praying, he heard a clear voice in his heart:

"Go and protect the children!"

Automatically the friar opened the church door to see the children, running towards him out of breath, and in tears:

'The police are after us, hide us!"

He took them to the parish house and locked them in an empty room. He went out to the yard and ran into a policeman who asked him if he had seen the children. The friar replied that he had seen them, but, strangely enough the official did not wait for a reply and ran towards Bijakovići. Father Jozo returned to the parish house and listened again to his recorded conversation with the children. Suddenly the conversation appeared quite different to him. He realized that the children's words had quite a different meaning to him compared to what he understood during his first questioning. That was when his soul was opposed to the apparitions. Now he found a profundity and spiritual richness in every word, of which he had not been aware before.

While the children were still locked in the parish house and were praying for the apparition, Father Jozo went to the church to prepare himself for the Mass. Some of the great joy and tranquility that emanated from the visionaries had rubbed off on him regardless of the difficulties and harassments that they had suffered.

He announced that the children would not be coming to church. The church was crowded, there were so many people that they were crammed around the altar and Father Jozo could not even spread his arms while he was giving the blessing. A group of young men who came from Posušje was also there. When they returned home, they said that it was not the Father Jozo they had known, because he had never preached with such strength and power ... as he did that evening ...as if Jesus himself had talked through him.

After that day of 2nd July, Our Lady told the visionaries to pass on Her wish to the priests that the 6 o'clock Mass should remain a tribute to the apparitions.

A Ferocious Campaign against Medjugorje

On Insurrection Day, July 4th, Mikulić, a member of the Communist party of Yugoslavia, on the occasion of the annual partisan meeting at Montenegro strongly condemned the inhabitants of Medjugorje for what he considered clerical nationalist actions. Free transportation had been organized to the place where, during the war a great many Italians had died in battle. All Yugoslav newspapers reported the speech of this "well known" communist and how he strongly condemned "clerical nationalists", friars, visionaries and all the inhabitants of Medjugorje who were enemies of socialism and according to him preparing a counter-revolution! A crime that communists used to punish with death. Mikulićs speech marked the beginning of government persecution. The police started to threaten the visionaries' parents and relatives more seriously. They banned cars from approaching the church and everybody had to park a kilometer or two away so it was very silent around the church, which of course helped everyone to concentrate more deeply.

There were many Orthodox and Muslims who came from distant places. Many of them received grace. The Orthodox Vidoje suffered from violent stomach ache and he had not slept for nights. When he took a bath in flowers he had brought from the foot of the hill where the apparition was, he was healed. Magda, from the neighboring village, got rid of pains after contemplating in ecstasy the spinning cross on the Križevac Hill. During these days of grace, Mara from Lištica came, too. She had been on pilgrimages to various holy places, because of her troubles. She came to Medjugorje wailing: "Our Lady, I can't stand it any more. I plead for my recovery or my death!"

According to her statement given in the parish house, her pains disappeared instantly.

The visionaries had to keep changing the places of their mysterious meetings. Sometimes the apparitions occured in their own houses or at a relatives' or friends' or perhaps in secret places in the hills. Our Lady followed them everywhere and kept encouraging them. Marija's mother asked if Our Lady always walked with them. They replied that Our Lady did not walk but She glided from one place to another. Their relatives said that they were happy that Our Lady appeared in their house, on "that wall".

"What wall?" asked Vicka: "When Our Lady comes, the walls disappear. All barriers vanish. Endless heavenly space opens in front of us, and from the middle of that space Our Lady descends in the midst of immensly beautiful light."

From the very beginning there was a group of fifteen young people who started to pray together according to Our Lady's wishes. They gladly accepted any sacrifices to be made. They went to Apparitions Hill by night and prayed there. This was the origin of the prayer group that would later be lead by the visionary Ivan and that still exists nowadays. Holy Mass became very important to them. Our Lady invited them to say as many as three rosaries a day. Little Jakov wondered:

"O, mother, how can I possibly say so many rosaries?"

Sometimes, when it was possible, the little boy, along with the other visionaries, went to church as early as around five o'clock in the afternoon. On his way he met his class-mates who were playing football, and he sometimes wished he could play with them. But only for a moment. He would remember Our Lady, the maternal love She lavished on him and he would quicken his step, happy that he, too, could do something for Her through his prayers for Our Lady and spend as many as five hours in the church. Although he was only a little boy, he thought about Jesus who suffered for all of us and whom he had seen on the cross when the Holy Virgin gave them this vision. Not only he, but also the other visionaries were sorry for the slightest offence that they might have by chance given to Jesus. It was only through this vision that they had realized the importance of converting and prayer because Jesus still suffers for our sins. This is why the Holy Mother taught them to pray before the crucifix right from the beginning.

Their faith was now more deep and true. Prayer became their daily bread and the things that their parents and relatives had tried to teach them now became their reality.

Other children, assisted by supernatural forces, followed them in their movements. They lived their faith with the joy expressed in their sincere and beautiful prayers.

One day, Ivan's mother took his jeans to wash them, she emptied the pockets and found the rosary she had been looking for. It was used by Ivan to recite the rosary, alone or with his friends.

Old Jozo lived near Križevac in the houses that belonged to Vasilj families. He had been blind for four years after a paralysis then and had sores all over his hands. When he heard about the appearances of Our Lady, he exclaimed: "I will tell if it's the Holy Mother or not!", he asked his relatives to bring him back some herbs from the hill. He put them under his head. The next morning he told his wife to bring him some water and put the herbs in it. He was saying the Creed while he was washing his face with the water. As he dried his face with a towel he yelled:

"Oh, my God, I can see!"

"What? What can you see?"

"I can see you are barefooted, you're not wearing stockings!"

He rubbed his hands with the herbs and the sores disappeared. His wife rushed out to tell the neighbors about the miraculous recovery. They immediately went to church to thank Our Lady for Her exquisite grace.

The news about this extraordinary healing spread quickly, newspaper reporters arrived and wrote about the blind man who had recovered his sight. This infuriated the communists. They threatened to have the reporters sacked, because they had received precise orders not to write in favor of Medjugorje, but rather against it.

More people than ever swarmed into Medjugorje to witness what was happening. People of all religions came, as well as atheists from all six Yugoslav republics. They were unafraid and even defiant as the police took note of the license numbers of their cars as they entered the village. The more the authorities wrote the numbers the more pilgrims arrived to climb the hill of the sacred apparitions.

Ivanka with her father

Ivan, Jakov and Marija in ecstasy

One morning Father Jozo left the parish house to go to church to prepare for the morning Mass. There were several buses from Hungary and a lot of people around in the yard. Everybody was looking towards Križevac and, saying with one voice, that they saw Our Lady. Father Jozo did not even look at the hill. He entered the church feeling annoyed and displeased, and thought that this could not be Our Lady because She would surely not create any disturbance during Holy Communion. But, as he was leaving the vestry to begin Mass, his heart swelled on seeing that all the people outside had now entered the church.

The Bishop Believes in the Apparitions

The Bishop of Mostar, Monsignor Pavao Žanić, well known for his devotion to Our Lady, first as a priest and then as a bishop, had been on eleven pilgrimages, to Lourdes, Fatima and Syracuse, Italy. He accepted the news about the apparitions in his diocese with joy and surprise. He was personally interested in these events. He questioned the visionaries on the spot, one by one, in the presence of the friars.

It wasn't easy for the children to answer his questions, as he was a clerical authority, but he was very sensitive and kind and so he helped them relax in his presence. He wanted to know if they really had seen Our Lady; what She looked like and what She had said. Marija Pavlović made the strongest impression on the Bishop because of her extreme modesty she reminded him of St. Bernadette of Lourdes. He even asked her to recommend him to Our Lady. He questioned her alone, without friars being present.

He recommend the children to pray to the Virgin and to continue being good, humble and sincere.

Shortly after he had met the visionaries, the Bishop confided in Father Jozo:

"The authorities have called me for an "informative" meeting. They are angry because I am defending Medjugorje. They have told me that they will put me in prison if I continue to do so!"

"Father Bishop please be careful, we have to be very cautious. I myself do not understand what is happening here. It is best to wait and not to rush out into the open as we could harm both ourselves and our Church."

One evening, in mid July, Our Lady appeared to Jakov in his house, and told him to go to the church and tell the congregation to recite the rosary together. He rushed towards the door, but there was a policeman standing outside on guard and the little seer did not dare try to pass by him... The boy started to pray ... A few minutes later the policeman fell asleep, so Jakov jumped out of the window and ran off to the church. He crept through the people and hid under the altar. When the Mass ended he shook Father Jozo's habit and whispered that he had a message. Father Jozo lifted him up on to the altar and little Jakov said loudly:

"Recite the rosary, recite it together!"

While little Jakov was speaking, a hush fell on the church. As soon as he finished speaking, the people - moved to tears - started to take out their rosaries. Father Jozo, still feeling a little reticent, did not allow his emotion to overwhelm him. But he too, took out his rosary and started praying. At the end of the prayer everyone realized that Father Jozo had suddenly stopped speaking and was staring above the third bench. His face was lit up with joy and ecstasy. After a few seconds, he began to sing: "Beautiful You are, Virgin Mary", and then beaming with happiness he concluded the rosary. It was only to a few of his closest friars that he admitted that he had also seen Our Lady in the church for a moment and that She had thanked him for following the invitation to prayer and asked him to continue reciting the rosary every evening, together with the congregation.

A few days later, during an apparition in the church, Our Lady told the visionaries:

"Do not "recite" the rosary but think about it in your heart and before you pray you must forgive your neighbours."

Friar Jozo conveyed the message to the congregation. Everyone stopped still and quiet. A man burst into tears and brimming with happiness exclaimed:

"I forgive my neighbour!" His intolerance and dislike which had weighed like a chain around his neck melted away.

Many others received the grace of forgiveness, they cried, hugged each other, forgave each other. During the day that followed, neighbours who were on bad terms and had not spoken for years, approached each other in the fields, shook hands, made peace and all five villages were united as never before.

One of these evenings towards dusk, a huge inscription appeared in the evening sky above Križevac. It was a short word in gold: MIR (PEACE). Many in the village clearly saw this as well as about a hundred people ten kilometers away from Medjugorje. An old woman, who was among them, saw only fire burning in the sky. She could not read because she was illiterate. Even Friar Jozo saw it. He described the phenomenon in the following words: a river of fire suddenly came down from the sky above Križevac, everyone thought Doomsday was coming, but, suddenly, this great fire became a word: PEACE. The inscription was clearly seen for a good ten minutes.

At that point it was no longer possible to stop people from coming to Medjugorje, to stop them from going up the

Podbrdo Hill, to besiege the visionaries' houses day and night. People came from all parts of the country and from abroad. The Orthodox people asked where the Mother of God had appeared, while the Muslims searched the place where the Mother of Pergamer (the prophet), Jesus, had appeared.

All the pilgrims made their wishes and pleas, they wrote them on pieces of paper, in Latin and Cyrillic scripts and gave them to the visionaries to forward them to Our Lady. The oldest of the visionaries could read the Cyrillic script, as it was compulsory study in schools at the time. They read these pleas, and relayed them to Our Lady everyday.

Pilgrims arrived at Bijakovići in the early morning. Vicka used to stand on the balcony of her house for hours and speak to the people about Our Lady's beauty, and how She loves them all and considers them Her children, and how She calls everyone to prayer, fasting, reconciliation and conversion.

A little Eastern Orthodox Christian boy was healed and a Catholic priest, who was there, was scandalized. The visionary Marija shocked by such a narrow minded attitude, asked Our Lady if She had a message for this priest. The answer was:

"It is you yourselves, who divide people on earth, who divided yourselves! You are all my children and God loves you all."

Although not all people left written testimony of what they experienced in Medjugorje, it can be said, without any exaggeration, that every one of them had a similar experience to a nun, who wishes to remain anonymous, who stayed in the visionary Marija Pavlović's house.

Not only did the nun have the opportunity to meet Marija personally but she realized just how modest and pious the girl was, and how it was through this seemingly normal girl that Our

Lady calls us all to follow the path of holiness by watching over each and every one of us regardless of who we are and where we came from. This same nun prayed with Marija, and one night at about 2 o'clock she went with all the visionaries up the hill and Our Lady asked them to repent and pray for others.

Before going to sleep in Marija's house, the nun listened to people passing by going up the hill in the night, singing:"

"O, Mother Mary how beautiful You are".

The same nun witnessed, along with several other people, the apparition that occurred in little Jakov's house. Shortly after the visionaries had stopped praying and were deep in silence, Vicka took a girl by her hand and helped her to touch the Invisible Virgin Mary.

Marija asked the nun if she wanted to do the same.

She did, but she neither saw nor felt anything while her hand was touching the Holy Mother. After the apparition the children sang: "To Your name, o Christ.." and they all set off for church.

It was only shortly after, while the nun was going towards the church along with the visionaries, that she suddenly became aware of what had happened within her:

"Every valley was filled ... every hill and mountain was straightened out. Crooked paths became straight".

She experienced something similar to what is described in Luke's Gospel, Chp. 3, verse 4:

"Prepare you the way of the Lord, make His paths straight!"

Many others had similar experiences; they saw clearly in themselves and said:

"My eyes are unveiled and now I can see clearly who I am and where I belong'."

Feed the Hungry, Give Water to the Thirsty

From the early morning in those days, there was a never-ending crowd of people thronging up the Podbrdo Hill. They climbed up in spite of the unbearable heat: it was 35°C in the shade! Women in high-heeled shoes, took their shoes off and continued uphill barefooted. There were many hardships for the first pilgrims who, hungry and thirsty, stood under the burning sun for hours, waiting to see the visionaries at the moment of the apparition. After it ended they went downhill to the village asking for water to drink. The peasants did their best ... They gave them everything they had: water, wine, bread and fruit as well.

There was no water supply system in Medjugorje. The people drank rain water from the water tanks and this soon ran dry. The peasants had to buy the water which was delivered in lorries. My relatives, who lived near the bridge, laid some pipes on the road connected to the tank to quench the thirst of those on the road. Marinko Ivanković from Bijakovići bought seven lorry loads of water and gave it to the people free of charge. During an apparition, Our Lady asked the visionaries to call Marinko to see Her. She embraced him in a sisterly way saying that few people were like him.

People who came from distant places needed lodgings for the night but there were no guest rooms in the peasants' houses. Nevertheless, the parishioners welcomed guests in their houses. When the houses were overcrowded people slept in the yards, on the balconies or in the gardens. This was not hard for the pilgrims because it was summer and hot. Even the visionaries' houses were full of pilgrims too. Very few had a bathroom in the house and they used the latrines in the yard. Jakov lived with his mother in a little room which was also the kitchen. Their guests slept at their front door and in the yard. Nobody locked the doors. All the houses were open, it never even occured to the inhabitants of Bijakovići or the other villagers nearby to charge their guests for the food and lodgings. They were very happy to be able to do something for those who came and they shared their happiness during these first weeks of the apparitions.

Jakov's mother worked by the day in a neighbour's field.

A priest from Zagreb came to little Jakov's house. The priest put some money under the tablecloth when little Jakov was not looking. But, Jakov noticed, took the money and returned it to the priest because he did not want to take any money ... not even to help his mother.

My relatives told me that one unforgettable evening a Gipsy tribe knelt in front of the church. This was not the only surprise for those who were there during those very special days. Some also saw an elderly Muslim crawling on his knees from the bridge to the church. Although most of the people who arrived at Medjugorje came to discover the hidden secrets in their hearts and souls, there were also those who came by virtue of duty, namely the secret police. The police watched what was happening very carefully eager to unmask what they imagined was the friars' deception. The Parish Priest was well aware that he was under the police surveillance and he taped all his sermons.

It turned out that his intuition was correct. The police accused him of antisocialist behaviour following his sermon of the 11th July. The following is a part of the sermon which Father Jozo gave that day ...

"The only one who came to tell us the truth was a God-man, Jesus Christ. He did not come to say "I've discovered the truth" but He said "I am the truth!" Jesus arrived among the lost children of God. He said "The spirit of the Lord is in me. This is why He annointed me and sent me to announce the good news: to free all prisoners, make the blind see, the deaf hear, the dumb speak and the lame to walk ... The spirit of the Lord God is upon me. He sent me to proclaim freedom for all slaves, freedom from prison and to announce the year of the Lord's Grace ..." Jesus came to free me ... a slave ... you ... a slave ... for you have lived in slavery all these forty years. He came so that you could kneel before Him and say unlock these chains, untie these knots which shackle my life because until now I've been a slave to my sins. Only you have the key!

Also this evening He will open the eyes of the blind ... and yours too ... No one should be so blind that they do not see ... No one should be so deaf that they do not hear this message and no one should be so selfish as not to give their love to everyone."

The Feast of St. James

On the eve of the Feast of St. James, the Parish Patron that blessed year in 1981, preparations were more intensive than ever before. The excitement was considerable, Our Lady had appeared among them and the children were preparing for the sacrament of Holy Confirmation. People painted their houses, rugs were washed and left to dry in the yards. Cakes were made on the eve of 25th July and food such as roastlamb, salami, cheese and prosciutto was prepared to offer generously to their friends and relatives coming to visit them. On that day the Holy Mass was celebrated in the grove near the school. Ringing bells announced the beginning of the Mass celebrated by the Bishop of Mostar.

During the Confirmation given by the Bishop, the inhabitants of Medjugorje expected to hear his opinion regarding the recent happenings in the parish. The Bishop did not disappoint them. Here is what he said in his sermon:

"I am convinced that the children have not been incited into saying that they have seen Our Lady. Had it been a case of only one child, you could perhaps have said that it was a tough child that did not confess to the police! But ... Six innocent, modest children would certainly have confessed everything if someone had put them up to it! I assure you that no priest has any part in all of this and neither has any priest encouraged them in this affair! ... I am also convinced that the children are telling the truth. Yet, the most difficult question remains: is this a supernatural experience of the children or not? May I remind you of what wise old Gamaliele said when the Jews wanted to prevent the apostles from speaking about Jesus: "If these are men's deeds they will fall to ruin, on the other hand, if these are God's deeds, no one can stop them...!"

These words encouraged the parishioners to persist in protecting the children and to follow the Virgin's messages communicated to the visionaries. These same words however enraged the communists; who immediately summoned all the party members of the surrounding villages threatening to expel anyone who went on Podbrdo Hill to witness the apparitions.

Once again the police harassed the visionaries even more vigorously, they even put a pistol to their temples threatening to kill them if they did not stop talking about their visions of Our Lady. These poor children were subject to derision and insults which developed into vulgar, unrepeatable obscenities towards their mothers.

Procession with the statue of St. James. Bishop Žanić is present in the second row

Their relatives also had a hard time, they shivered with fear at the mere sight of a policeman! Marija's mother Iva had even more reasons to be afraid than the others because several years earlier she had suffered a frightening experience at their hands. She had been taking the sheep to pasture with a woman from the neighboring village. When she returned home, the police were waiting for her and they took her away to prison. Here they questioned and tortured her in order to make her confess that she had met up with Croatian dissidents in the mountains. Denial was of no use. They locked her in a room, without food and water for two days. She slept on the bare floor and there was no toilet. Iva had been reported by the woman who was with her in the mountains because a policemen had talked her into false witness in exchange for a washing machine!

This is why Iva was more careful than the others and she advised them to watch their words because the enemy was dangerous and powerful. She warned her husband Filip not to drink too much because a word too many could cause trouble for everybody. He told her not to worry because if he were to become a little tipsy the worst he would do would be to burst into song to the glory of the Holy Mother. Let the police listen to that! Filip worked hard to support his six children, in the past he used to shout at them, but now he had became very patient, humorous and courageous. The thing that made him most happy was that Our Lady appeared to his daughter every day.

On the other hand, Iva kept asking Marija lots of questions. She told her to touch Our Lady's dress to see if it were made like theirs, "No mother, it isn't" replied Marija, "It's not like our cloth, my fingers slip from it as if it were silk!" Whenever she asked Marija what Our Lady had said, her daughter told her to pray and Iva would answer:

"I do, my child, I have recited the rosary since I can remember, I pray in the fields and when I'm with the sheep."

"I know mother but even more, it won't do any harm!"

Also my parents, the Vasilj's, discussed all the events that were taking place. My cousin Peško, who was fifty, was rather a doubting Thomas at first. But, after the first few days of the visions, he changed attitude telling everyone that he knew where he belonged; that he saw what man could not do and that on one occasion he had even seen the Blessed Virgin Mary taking leave of the children. My fifteen-year old cousin Jelena, at the very first Mass felt something dissolve inside: something which had stopped her feeling near to God. She did not previously listen to the sermon but now she deeply experienced and absorbed every word. Her father explained to the rest of our family how, through prayer, the inspiration of the Holy Spirit had come helping them to become better people.

Thirty-five-year old Grgo maintained that it would take hours and hours to talk about everything. He saw his own faults clearly and the more he went to church the more he was able to correct himself. "That's why we must go to church!" he explained. Grgo realized that we should not be "part-time" devotees to God but go to church even when one "had no time!" to pray ... to help ourselves ... pray much more than ever before.

He told his family that from that moment onwards they should all grow in faith for they were all highly blessed but unaware of it ... He remembered how, just after the war, anyone taking the Lord's name in vain would be slapped by those who heard the swearing ... while now swearing and cursing were "one of the family". However, now that Our Lady had appeared, bad language was once again disappearing!

Speaking about cursing, I was told that the visionary Ivan Dragičević's grandfather had been a very devoted and pious man, he prayed continually: at home, at work in the fields ... everywhere. He had the best tobacco plants and he would share them with everyone. Those who wanted to get more than their fair share used to curse in front of him confident that he would say:

"God forgive, take everything, I can not listen to such blasphemy!"

He would run away immediately, leaving them all the fruits of his labours.

The women too, were happier now. They no longer heard the cursing of young teenagers gathered in front of the shops. It was wonderful how everybody changed for the better. If before the swearing had perhaps made them feel "more important", they now felt ashamed of their conduct and turned to discussing their prayers and faith.

They realized too that other teenagers, from other villages nearby, would listen carefully to what they had to say and to their advice.

The Fruits of the Conversion

Twenty-year old Ante from Bijakovići realized that before the apparitions he had enjoyed too much freedom, which got him into trouble with his friends. Before the apparitions he used to show off in front of the girls ... After he never failed to attend Mass first and foremost ... before anything else ... He no longer wasted time flirting around with the first girl he met up with or invite her to stay out all night with him.

Draženka who was the same age as Ante confirmed that also the girls had changed their behaviour and were now good, polite young ladies.

The older people noticed all these changes. They were amazed how easily they had stopped quarrelling and how tolerant they had become. How happy they were in their hearts to "let things be" by not holding anything against other people; there was no trace of hate in them for others.

Eighty-year old Zlatan, born at the beginning of the twentieth century admitted frankly:

"I remember everything I got up to in my life, and so I pray to God for people I offended in the past. And for a few women that I deceived and who are now dead."

Fifty-year old Ivan added: "We did not lose anything because of prayer. If anybody had told me that we would have prayed like this before Our Lady had appeared I would have said: "I can not live like this!" – yet, there is time for everything, we give everything to the people that come here and we have everything for ourselves, thank God!"

Another fifty-year old man, Ante, joined the conversation:

"Even if Our Lady were not to appear anymore a great change has taken place. Something has happened. We've all got closer. There are no quarrels any more. It seems to me that every one of us is happy: we are happy with what we have, we do not need anything else. We no longer show off in front of each other and we've found time for everyone! Now we have time for everything!"

Old Pero remarked:

"There has always been respect and help towards everyone here: if anyone was in need we would make a help collection in the parish. Yet, there is more harmony and peace now and our relationships are better. Even more so to pilgrims."

Toše, who was about forty, hosted hundreds of people and many of them admitted that they themselves could not have done the same for the inhabitants of Medjugorje. These pilgrims were unaware of what was obvious to all the parishioners: by sparing no efforts they gained much more than they had given away to the pilgrims.

Father Žarko Ilić, editor of "The homeland", an anthology published annually in Hercegovina, wrote that he had experienced the gatherings of the people as a People's University of Faith and Prayer.

A complete and total conversion was requested first to the inhabitants of Medjugorje who luckily, you could say, responded to the invitation whole-heartedly. In return they received great spiritual gifts. This is why they were privileged to bear witness to Our Lady's presence there. Two students from the village lived in Mostar, hosted by a Muslim family, they were preparing for their summer exams. The Muslim husband and wife used to quarrel often. Rasim, the husband, said to his wife: "We must stop quarrelling, look at these boys, look how nice they are and polite! Compared to them we are like animals."

Priest Marijan Ljubić, who was among the first to publish a book on the apparitions in German, reflected carefully on the numerous supplications and questions that the visionaries made to the Madonna at the beginning. He concluded that one of the purposes of so many apparitions was Our Lady's wish to answer as many as possible of "Her children's" questions and to induce a wish in all of us to address Her with their same trust. If we cannot always address Her

Pilgrims queue for the confession

through the visionaries, we can address Her through our devoted prayer, which She has always recommended.

After the first several thrilling weeks, the inhabitants of Medjugorje stopped asking questions, not because they did not have any more questions, but because they found the answers in their prayer and because their meeting with Jesus, during evening Mass, became the most important thing to them. There might be urgent jobs to do in the fields, but they would leave everything and rush to church to meet God in the Eucharist. The visionaries often led the rosary before the apparition. Suddenly, in the middle of the prayer, the children would fall silent while the people would hold their breath. Everybody knew that Our Lady was among them. The mother of one of the visionaries clearly saw Her three times hovering above the benches. She revealed it to her daughter, who told her not to tell anyone about this apparition and to thank Our Lady for appearing to her thus giving her the strength to endure all the persecutions she and others had been suffering along with the children.

After the first ten apparitions, most of which were carefully taped, others followed, which were recorded in the memories of the visionaries. Many times the harassed children met with Our Lady by themselves in some hidden place on Podbrdo. Here they were not burdened with hundreds of pilgrims' pleas and questions. In that period the Holy Virgin appeared several times a day. Their relatives told me of how they would suddenly kneel down in the house and communicate with the Madonna. As soon as the apparition ended, they would return to their jobs as if nothing had happened. Only their eyes shone with a strange light that seemed to reflect the skies with which they had just been in contact.

Five of the visionaries: Mirjana, Vicka, Marija, Ivanka and Ivan were mostly on hand for the pilgrims and repeated the Holy Mother's message to them. Jakov however avoided all of this. When the apparitions occurred in the church, he would immediately disappear afterwards. He could not wait to get out into the fresh air. It was difficult to breathe because of the heat and so many people. Little Jakov figured out the simplest solution: let Our Lady appear to everybody, so people would leave him alone and everybody would know that he is not lying.

During an apparition in a hidden place in the mountains, Ivanka asked Our Lady about her mother again and wanted to know if her mother needed prayers or Masses. The answer was:

"Your mother is well, she does not need anything..."

While She was speaking Ivanka's mother appeared near Our Lady, all in white with a veil on her head. The girl saw Her as if She had been in flesh and blood. First Our Lady kissed Ivanka and then her mother did the same, she smiled at her without a saying word and let her know that she was pleased with her.

Ivan, Marija, Ivanka, Mirjana, Jakov and Vicka

Towards the end of July, Our Lady started to greet the visionaries with:

"Praised be Jesus!"

They asked Her again if She would leave them a sign. She said that She would, but that they would have to be patient:

"My sweet angels, even when I have left a sign many will not believe all the same and they will only come to see ... People must change. They must be converted and do penance."

They often asked Her about help for the many sick people. The Blessed Virgin Mary told them:

"Without faith, nothing is possible. All those who believe firmly will be cured. God can do anything."

Whenever they could, on every occasion, in church or at home, the visionaries recommended people to follow Our Lady's messages, the most important are:

Peace - the first message, which was written in golden letters in the sky. Our Lady often warned the children of how the tensions between nations were only a step away from catastrophe. It was through them that She appealed to all of humanity to maintain peace and She explained that it is possible to stop war through prayer and fasting on the condition that there is peace in the heart which comes through prayer. Without peace in the heart it is not possible to pray for peace in the world. Peace will come if we surrender ourselves to prayer dedicated to Jesus allowing Him to guide us. Our Lady came to lead the entire world to Jesus.

Conversion - It is quite a frequent message of Our Holy Mother. She says that God is dead for a great many Christians. Many go to church out of habit; Christians should be an example to all those who do not believe in God. She also said: "Dear children, tell everybody that conversion lasts the entire life and you should pray to God for it".

Prayer - As early as in the second apparition Our Lady accepted and appreciated the prayers recited by the children: seven times "The Lord's Prayer", "Hail Mary" and "Glory Be" advising them to add the Creed, which She said was the best prayer. She invited them to tell everybody in the parish to say the rosary, not only in words, but with their hearts. As a preparation for the Eucharist, She taught them to say two rosaries before the Mass and another one as a thanksgiving after Mass because, as She repeatedly said to the children, people often forget to give thanks.

She explained that one could not live faith without prayer and She asked the visionaries to call the entire world to prayer. She also said that there were many believers who did not pray. She added that She needed their prayers and without them She would not able to fulfill the goal for which God had sent Her. As for those in bad health, She pointed out that many people should pray together for those who are seriously ill. Regarding personal prayer She instructed the visionaries to finish them in time so as not to be late for Holy Mass.

Fasting - It was mentioned for the first time when the visionaries were praying for the healing of little Daniel. The Holy Mother first remarked sadly that fasting had almost disappeared from the Church then She explained that a fast of just bread and water should be carried out every Friday.

The children realized that fasting, along with prayer, was the strongest means of conversion and the most powerful weapon against satan, who, at all times tries to mislead people into evil and to separate them from God. During one apparition Our Lady said that generally speaking, a fast could not be replaced by acts of charity. This is only allowed to those who are ill, accompanied with confession and Holy Communion.

Reconciliation - Our Lady did not talk much about this sacrament, as She had already done so, in other apparitions. She said however that the Church would "heal" better if believers confessed monthly.

Holy Mass - It should be the center of our life. It is here that we can meet Jesus who suffered and died for us and who is our Savior. From the beginning, She explained to the children that the Holy Mass was more important than Her apparitions. She told them to pray to the Holy Spirit for the renewal of the parish and that they should all attend Holy Mass with joy, in order to experience a true encounter with God. As before ... indifference means returning home empty hearted.

Conversion and penance is the theme of all the apparitions and therefore it is not by chance that Our Lady often appeared dressed in a grey dress, which is the symbol of penance. On several occasions She sent a message through the children to the priests inviting them to be firm in their faith, to cultivate their parishoners' faith and to act as the Church ordered them.

Many times Our Lady showed symbols during apparitions: a cross, a heart and a sun explaining:
"The cross is sign of your salvation."

"The heart is a symbol of God's love for you."

"The sun, the light is Jesus who enlightens your faith."

When She went away, these symbols would remain behind for a moment, sometimes there were inscriptions, too: "Peace! Peace to humanity!"

The visionaries watched the Holy Mother bless the people while holding various objects. Once She told them that She especially blessed a group of pilgrims who had come from Varaždin near Zagreb and because they were good Christians, She asked the children to tell them so.

In the meantime the secret police tried to intimidate Father Jozo by calling him for questioning. They threatened him to make him deny the existence of the Holy Mother and the apparitions. They wanted him to admit that the children suffered from hallucinations. He replied that he could not say that the children were liars just like that. He, Jozo, needed time and quiet to question the children thoroughly so that he could report it to the Church Authorities.

The Secrets

From the very beginning the children explained that Our Lady had promised to reveal ten secrets to each of them, and that they would, when the time came, relay these to the Church Authorities. After only a few weeks, Our Lady revealed five secrets to each of the visionaries which refer to some future events. The children have not spoken very much about them and the dates when Our Lady revealed these secrets is unknown. The only thing that the priests and relatives came to know was that the third secret would be a lasting, indestructible sign which would appear in the place of the apparitions, for everybody and especially for non-believers, to see. All six visionaries know which sign it will be, and four of them know the date on which it will appear. They explained that many miraculous healings would take place following to its appearance and that there would be little time left for conversion so it is essential to take advantage of this moment of grace now.

Nothing in the world could force the children to reveal anything more about the secrets which Our Lady told them. They are absolutely silent about what cannot and must not be told. Many people ask them questions about these secrets but their answer is always the same:

"A secret is a secret!".

The children don't know if these secrets, that they know, are the same for each of them or different ... because they keep them so well that they do not discuss them together. So that you can understand, I'd like to repeat what they themselves explained to me:

"Each one of us feels completely alone during the apparitions. Sometimes we hear what the others say ... sometimes we do not! We don't worry about this because the Blessed Mother doesn't say the same thing to each of us. We are just happy to be with Her and we are not surprised that She also speaks to all of us separately. This is God's will and everything is possible for Him."

Marija's mother has often asked her daughter what Our Lady has said, but she has learned nothing more than others have. The girl has deftly avoided her mother's traps and says with a gentle, mysterious smile:

"Pray, mother, pray, don't ask about the secrets, because secrets are secrets and they are a secret for you, too! You know that each of us has received five secrets. Our Lady promised to give us another five. When, we do not know ... maybe tomorrow, but maybe after many years as well. She will give them in the course of our lives, because She promised to. You know what, you could even die before we get all the secrets. So pray, Our Lady does not ask anything else of you!"

During the first weeks of the apparitions, Our Lady encouraged the children by saying:

"I know that many will not believe you, I know that many who are enthusiastic now will cool off later, but you must persevere and never fail to urge the world not to stop praying, to do penance and to convert. In the end, you will be the happiest of all."

The visionaries were untiring in relaying the messages of Our Lady. They repeated them hundreds of times a day and they were happy that not only the entire parish accepted them whole-heartedly but most of the barefooted pilgrims, who were there in Medjugorje during these first exciting days. The church was full, the yard as well, right from the early afternoon. People waited for confession. Father Jozo invited dozens of friars from the Humac monastery and other parishes to help him. For hours on end the priests were confessing people in the church, or outdoors in the meadows. They were amazed at this divine turn of events!

There were people that had not entered a church for more than thirty, forty years who started to attend Mass. Atheists, who had forgotten that they had ever been baptized, felt deep, sincere remorse, and confessed freely their past mistakes. They would leave with their eyes full of tears of joy after receiving the indulgence through Christ's servant.

There were quite a few really extraordinary inspirations of faith. These are examples: a man who cursed heavily, stopped this bad habit after he had confessed. A clerk, inspired by Our Lady's call, turned from being an aggressive and quarrelsome person to a humble believer who used to say as many as four rosaries a day. A drunk, who had not been able to give up this vice, suddenly stopped drinking.

Nobody will ever be able to tell of all those touching events related to the conversions. One should have been in Medjugorje in those days, in the houses, with the people. Conversion was in the air you breathed. Nobody cooked on Fridays, because they fasted on bread and water. The same in the nearby parishes and even farther away in the places from where barefooted pilgrims came. In many canteens, even in Mostar, many people did not touch their food during the lunchtime break. Miners from Bosnia fasted, too.

It was summer. The people arrived hot and weary at the crossroads of Tromedja then they had to go up a narrow track where cars got stuck. However nobody yelled or cursed. People went to and from the church like a peaceful river, flows in its bed. Prayer and penance spread among individuals and also among the entire groups as well. When they sang in church they were in perfect harmony like a perfect choir. Even those who had never sung before, because they had not a musical ear, started singing too.

One night Vicka communicated the following message from the Blessed Virgin:

"Dear children, thank you for answering my call. Live my messages, because if you do not live them you will not be able to communicate them to others. When you return home, don't talk about what you experienced here, unless you are asked. Your words will be in vain, words themselves will not open the hearts of your dear ones. Live these messages in your houses and pray in silence for your relations as only this will give fruits."

The national television kept accusing the Parish Priest, Father Jozo and the visionaries of being "dangerous counter-revolutionaries" from Medjugorje. They showed subversive inscriptions on the hill, which, they themselves had written. They showed some young men, who were disguised agents, singing nationalist songs. Cartoons of Our Lady were published in the newspapers and a TV crew came from Sarajevo to film the children. Vicka, Marija, Ivan and Jakov hid themselves because they were sure these men wanted to ridicule them and their visions.

In order not to return to their editors empty handed, some of the reporters looked for old Jozo Vasilj who had recovered his sight by Our Lady's Grace. They bothered him with many questions, insinuating that he had not really been blind all along and that he must have invented everything to become famous. The old man resented this and consequently refused to allow anybody else in his house if they wanted to question him.

Strange Signs in the Sky

On one of these memorable summer evenings, Our Lady invited the children to go to a certain place on Podbrdo Hill rather late in the evening. They went accom-panied by about forty relatives and friends. When they reached the spot, they knelt and started praying. Suddenly the sky opened, an immense light shone upon the entire hill while a luminous kind of globe appeared falling gently towards the children; before it touched the ground, it burst into a thousand stars. The light was seen by many people who were on the other side of the village. That night the apparition lasted for over forty minutes.

The next day, hundreds of pilgrim watched the Sun setting and excited shouts could be heard from everywhere:

"The Sun! The Sun! Look at the Sun!"

The Sun could easily be looked at with the naked eye, it was bigger than usual, completely white and very bright. It was spinning fast, first to the right and then to the left it seemed to be swinging. Powerful waves of light radiated from the Sun. Wider and wider rays appeared, milky white and glittering, they extended progressively; some of them disappeared in the sky and some descended to the ground and just before they touched the ground they seemed to bend towards the church and above the people. The pilgrims were afraid of this powerful light that suddenly descended towards them. They knelt in prayer. Immediately after that, it was noticed that the Sun was surrounded by a red ring, which became golden after a few moments. Then, everything was as before and nobody could look at the burning summer sun without sunglasses.

As soon as the vision ended somebody yelled:

"Look at the cross on Križevac!"

A kind of red haze appeared around the cross, which then took the form of a heart; the cross was clearly seen inside. The red heart slowly left the cross and descended almost to the foot of the hill, then it came up again and surrounded the cross. Again a few moments later the heart turned into a large image of Our Lady with Her hands spread out and Her head bowing. This was also seen by two old priests, Father Stanko Vasilj and Father Janko Bubalo, who made a written and signed statement.

*Pilgrims observe the play of the sun. The image of Our Lady on
the Votive Cross, remains stamped on the film*

In those days Heaven was on the Earth and many claimed to see great globes of light. My uncle Janko told me that he and our parents and neighbours had seen a great globe of light above the Apparition Hill before midnight. It stood over the hill for a long time. My grandaunt Anica sadly noted that everybody had seen this and that some had seen angels, some had seen globes yet, she had "only" seen Our Lady with the little Jesus in Her hands!

Apart from oral testimonies, there are photographs, too. Doctor Skritek from Croatia took pictures of the Apparition Hill. He made several photographs from different angles. When he developed the film, the photos showed the silhouette of a woman with a veil covering her head instead of the scenery of the hills. This sign inspired him and his family to a better Christian life.

Another woman, Šima, told me that one day she was in the fields working the vineyard when, at a certain point, she thought she saw Our Lady about a hundred meters away. She ran to see "Her" better and realized that it was just a withered poplar tree, bleached by the Sun. She was mistaken and there was nothing strange in that, because she had been working hard for quite a long time, and when she looked up, she saw something white in the distance. Her wish to have a vision too, conjured up the image of Our Lady. Instead it was only a withered old tree without its bark, bleached white by the sun. While she was telling me about this she added:

"You know, I am not sorry to say that I had no "vision" and I'm not sorry I never saw Our Lady. The most important thing for me is how I felt in my heart during those first days. Nobody can persuade me that they are not true … the visions that is … Paradise was here on the Earth. My heart was thrilled. An intimate kind of warmth and pleasure filled me. They harassed us, threatened us, but we all felt as safe as we were children in a mother's arms. Mirjana, you should have been here during those first days; people passed by our houses day and night heading towards Križevac, they were saying rosaries and singing Our Lady's songs. Hundreds of them spent the night in our house. People came from all over the country and we hosted them as if they had been our brothers. We could not wait for evening to fall and attend the Holy Mass. We never felt tired. Everybody speaks about a sign. What can be a more significant sign than all these people who have been coming here, and still come, in summer and in winter, day after day?"

Like her, I imagine that others too have suffered hallucinations, but it is understandable, normal and human. Who can say with absolute certainty what the pilgrims actually saw and what they imagined?

Hundreds of people claimed and testified in writing that they had seen the cross on Križevac suddenly disappear and that nobody could see it for fifteen minutes and than it reappeared. This event was seen in the morning and in the evening, be it rain or sunshine, often the cross spun round and round, and sometimes it looked like a slim white figure of Our Lady with Her hands spread wide. Other times the cross turned in various directions, the upper bar of the cross would disappear making the cross look T-shaped - (tau - the sign of salvation). In these moments, it would be very bright.

Here I must mention that my cousin Zdravka, who, as early as before the II World War, when she was ten, used to watch the cross turn on its axel. Sometimes the vertical trunk seemed to disappear and the cross became luminous. This was before the children's visions and the apparitions so she could not have been influenced by anything at all. She did not talk about it to anybody and she remembered the event when she came back to her hometown Medjugorje and discovered that the very same phenomenon was now seen by hundreds of people. This indirectly confirms one of Our Lady's messages given to the children:

"It is true that some pilgrims see me beside the cross. The cross was a part of the God's plan for this parish!"

Oceans of Grace

While in those days of grace, peoples' hearts were thrilled with joy because the Heavens had come so close to the Earth, Father Jozo was ever more deep in thought and more and more worried.

As a priest, he was obliged to consider the events with reserve and detachment and give his opinion on the basis of which the Church would decide if and which further actions should be undertaken.

As a man, he was immensely happy for he, too, had seen Our Lady, not only once, but three times .... he had experienced the immense love that Our Lady holds for the priests. She said:

"Certain people do not like their priests. Say the rosary, believe firmly and defend the Church. Live the Holy Mass!"

As had happened to many pilgrims, Friar Jozo realized from the bottom of his heart that Our Lady was not only a woman who was seen by the visionaries and who talked to them, but She is and was an ocean of grace. Her messages are seeds that carry life and inspire to conversion. She protects us all as if we were Her own children. Her words create new situations, She fills our hearts with grace and illumines everything. The Holy Mother has opened our eyes and has taught us how to reconcile with God. Medjugorje proceeds like a river: a river that purifies and cleanses giving life wherever it flows. Thus Medjugorje invited us to purify and cleanse our human relationships and relations with the Church in order to raise both to a service of mutual love.

Being aware of this, Friar Jozo allowed the visionaries to relay Our Lady's messages directly to the people. In these messages it was said that satan was strong and victory over him can only be won through prayer and fasting. Friar Jozo did not miss any opportunity to inspire people to pray for their enemies and for those who have never heard of Christ. By now he had become a firm supporter of the children and their relatives, too. Marija's mother experienced it when she asked him:

"Father, what will become of our children?"

"Don't be afraid Iva, we are on God's side!"

The visionaries lived their lives: they continued working on the tobacco plantations and in the vinyards. They did not feel tired and their only thoughts were their daily meeting with Our Lady. They were careful to hide from the police and they returned home late in the evening using mountain paths known only to them. The pilgrims were always waiting for them at their houses, and they continually repeated the beautiful story about Our Holy Mother of all men who came for each and every one of us. Vicka, who was the most eloquent, confided to those who were in her house:

"If you only knew how good Our Lady is, how She understands us". We asked Her how long She would stay with us and She replied: "As long as you want, my angels!" Do you understand..... as long as we want!? And we would like Her to stay with us forever. We are willing to go in to prison for Her, if necessary, we would die for Her. Only Our Lady knows our sufferings and how much more we may have to suffer. A little we already know, but She comforts us by telling us that we have finished all our trials. What will happen will happen! It's enough to see Her once and all sufferings vanish!"

Before the end of the first month of the apparitions, Our Lady met the chosen ones several times a day and asked them to pray for special purposes. Once She said:

"Stay little Jakov, you others can go!"

No one has ever known what Our Lady told Jakov when they remained alone and why She asked him to stay with Her. He was as firm as a rock in keeping his secret. On the other hand, when Our Lady had a particular remark to make regarding the visionaries, She would speak directly to the one it referred to, while the others did not hear anything. Her admonition was full of love and understanding.

During one of the apparitions Our Lady told the children that She had come to glorify Her Son who had suffered so much for humanity. As if in a movie She showed them Jesus covered in blood, His face covered with spittle. After that apparition they all cried because of the suffering of their Savior. On an other occasion they saw Jesus again who told them: "You must have a firm faith in me. Pray ... do not fear, my angels. Persevere and you will win!"

The visionaries asked Our Lady the questions put forward by the people. She did not always give an answer; sometimes She was silent, sometimes She sang with Her angelic voice, but most often She prayed. Those present could hear what the visionaries were saying but not what Our Lady replied. She told them to be cautious, careful and not to worry about the questions of certain persons including a priest. When the authorities gave a sealed envelope to the visionaries telling them to ask Our Lady what was in it, She replied that it contained nothing and advised the children to avoid this kind of game in the future. Infinite times the children repeated the Holy Mother's message that there is only one God ... that She herself has arrived to help the people, through prayer, in Her plan to convert humanity.

She frequently repeated that She was Mother of all people, not only of the Catholics, to whom She advised to love their brother Muslims, Orthodox and atheist who governed the country. When people asked them if Our Lady takes particular care for Catholics in a special way, they replied decisively:

"She has never said us dear Catholic children!"

The enormous grace that embraced the entire parish helped the inhabitants of Medjugorje to understand this message and sincerely rejoice at being with people of other religions, but also for the conversion of those atheists whose heart was touched and converted by the Mother's call. Those who once denied God, now knelt together with the villagers and the other pilgrims in the church, faces lit with joy. There were many old members of the Communist party and their presence confirmed the truthfulness of the apparitions.

The inhabitants of Medjugorje and Bijakovići showed understanding for the police realizing that they were there by virtue of their duty and so to make their job easier they helped them by keeping order around the church and the access roads.

After Mass, prayers were programmed as follows: the Creed, seven Lords Prayer's, seven Hail Mary's and seven

Glory Be and a prayer for the sick. One evening there was a university professor's wife from Sarajevo, an Orthodox, Olivera. She had three traffic accidents and her left arm was completely paralyzed. During the Mass, she felt a kind of warmth all over her body and the sensation of an electric shock through her arm. She was cured that same evening and she left a written statement to the friars.

A group of Italians who were spending their vacation by the sea, came one day to the church square, because they heard that something strange was going on. They met Father Jozo in front of the church and bombarded him with questions. He did not understand them so he just smiled and shrugged his shoulders showing that he was sorry he was not able to talk with them. They left looking puzzled and perplexed. Who knows what they had experienced while they were there!

The Struggle for the Souls

On the fortieth day of the apparitions, 2nd August, the visionaries Vicka, Marija, Jakov, Ivan and Mirjana were in the church, Mirjana had returned from Sarajevo in the meantime. Ivanka was still in Mostar. As soon as Our Lady appeared, She showed them Paradise, where they saw, among others, Ivanka's mother. It was like a film, the visionaries told the people that were gathered there:

"Our Lady showed us Paradise so that we could tell you it does exist and that it is a reward for those who follow God's Will."

A great many people set off to Podbrdo Hill after the Mass that evening and remained there all night praying and singing. When Marija returned home that night, Our Lady appeared to Her again and said:

"There is a great struggle between my Son and satan. It is the battle for the souls. Satan wants to insinuate himself between you to divide you ... you must resist him. Come all together to the Gumno field this evening."

Marija, Ivan, Mirjana and Jakov started out, followed by about fifty people, for the Gumno field. When Our Lady appeared She told the children to tell the people that everybody there might touch Her. As soon as some of them touched Her dress the visionaries noticed that they dirtied it. Our Lady disappeared and Marija cried:

A view of Medjugorje 1981

"Oh my God, what a terrible thing, Our Lady has gone away with a dirty stained dress!"

None of the visionaries remembers whose hands stained Our Lady's dress. This shows the educative role of the Heavenly Mother; because She let them know that She had been touched by sinful people but She did not allow them to identify them. Marinko, who was there, invited everyone to confession the next day.

Only two days later, the Parish Priest, Father Umberto Lončar of Gradnići, a village nearby Medjugorje along with several other people, saw a beautiful woman gliding through the skies towards the church of Medjugorje. They all made a written statement of this extraordinary event.

Under pressure by the Communist party of Yugoslavia, meetings were summoned at various levels in the Čitluk Municipality. The members assembled there exclaimed: "Those of you who have only been once to the hill of the apparitions, will be forgiven and it will be as if nothing happened! Those instead, who have been twice, will receive a public reprimand. Those who have been three times however, will be expelled from the Communist party".

Every member at the meeting had to declare the number of times they had visited the hill. One young man admitted nine visits and added: "You'll have to expel me three times!"

The authorities invented any excuse to call the friars to account, accusing them of subversive activities.

By mid August, the police summoned about two hundred inhabitants of Medjugorje to the school in order to persuade them that the friars were playing games with them and told them stories for little children thus distracting them from their work in the fields. An indignant old man reacted immediately: "I get up at dawn, I sing as I work, I attend Mass every evening and yet, my fields are tidy, I'm not behind with my work, can you say the same for your fields?"

A university professor tried to persuade these people that the signs they had seen in the sky were nothing but mere hallucination. Ivan Ivanković (Vicka's elder cousin), an ex student of the professor replied very firmly that everything they had seen was absolutely true. This energetic answer cost him two months in prison.

Other people who maintained the truth of the signs in the sky were also convicted for two months!

The national television kept accusing the friars, the visionaries and all the inhabitants of Medjugorje as "bitter enemies of the state".

The newspapers wrote articles with the following headlines: "The visionaries dark games!", "Where does Our Lady come from?", "The Holy Mother invented by Friars!"

Of course every article they wrote contained a warning to the people against the extremely dangerous clerical-nationalists from Hercegovina alluding to Father Jozo Zovko and Father Ferdo Vlašić, editor of the "Our Homeland" magazine. They distorted the words and expressions used during sermons, trying to create negative opinions about the friars in order to gain public support and legitimize their repressions.

The authorities feared the reaction of the workers returning from abroad for Assumption Day, August bank holiday. Orders were given from Belgrade to put down the subversive movement in the Republic of Bosnia and

Hercegovina, this "Rebellion" being called "Our Lady Movement".

Special forces from Sarajevo were sent to Medjugorje and they were ordered to shoot at the people. The village was surrounded and military forces were everywhere.

Access to the hills of Podbrdo and Križevac were banned and all the men from Medjugorje were ordered to go on duty watching the hills day and nigh so that no one could climb them.

The inhabitants of Bijakovići used to take their sheep to Podbrdo to pasture. Whether they liked it or not, they had to go up there.

Iva, the mother of Marija one of the visionaries, took her sheep to the place of the apparitions as usual. She noticed that the wooden cross had disappeared. Looking around she discovered that it had been flung in a ditch full of thorn bushes.

Without the least hesitation, she pulled it out and put it back in its place. Suddenly, a soldier appeared shouting:

"What are you doing here, don't you know that this area is forbidden?"

"How did you manage to see me?" asked Iva.

"I was down below on guard, my comrade saw you so he called me on the radio telling me to bring you in!" Very well' she replied. "You can take me to Zagreb and Belgrade if you want, I have never been there. It will make a change but ... if a wolf kills my sheep while I am away you will pay for it with interest!"

Iva was smart enough to persuade the soldier that she simply had to take the sheep to pasture. So he let her go and did not take her away!

Vicka's father, along with some other workers from the village, arrived from Germany on vacation. However they could not enjoy their holiday because they were in fear of having their passports confiscated. They returned to Germany before Assumption Day. His wife Zlata agreed because they lived in poverty and needed his "German salary" to survive.

In Bijaković and other villages, everybody pleaded to their patron St. James and Our Lady to save and protect their families. There was old Mara who tried to cheer everyone up by saying to her relatives: "Nobody is more protected than we are! The Madonna and the "military" are here!"

Another very old woman approached one of the armed men who was keeping watch under the hot sun and asked him kind-heartedly:

"My son, are you thirsty? Would you like some water?"

The soldier, an Orthodox, later told his relatives in Bosnia:

"They sent us to shoot at those people. I was keeping watch and I was hot and sweating when an old woman approached me offering me a drink of water. She looked like my grandmother. I almost cried!"

As early as at dawn, pilgrims from Hercegovina, Dalmatia and Bosnia arrived in cars or on foot for the celebrations. With rosaries in their hands, a flow of people crossed the barriers of soldiers who were keeping guard at the entrance to the village. Many were bare footed. Witnesses say that there were more than twenty thousand people attending the Holy Mass. A bus load of special agents with dogs arrived from

Sarajevo, and they wondered why they had been sent there because the people were passing by peacefully, praying and doing no harm. They wondered why many people were barefoot although it was obvious that they were not used to walking without shoes. They walked as if on hot coals, because the asphalt was burning hot. There was an "air of expectation".

After Assumption Day the inhabitants of Medjugorje gave a sign of relief as it seemed that the greatest danger was over and they could go back to their everyday jobs in the fields. So, there were only a few people in front of the church on that early morning of 17th August waiting for the Mass to begin. Suddenly the secret police from Belgrade, the 'UDBA', arrived in plain clothes. They asked the people to indicate Father Jozo. Some were silent, some told them that the priest was in the church. At that very moment Father Jozo came out from the church, they asked him, too:

"I am Father Jozo. What's the matter?" he asked.

"You must come with us!" they commanded.

They entered the vicarage, ordered him to change into ordinary clothes and shortly after took him out, handcuffed. The parishioners started crying when they saw him and the Parish Priest, pale faced, found the courage to say:

"Goodbye. May God be with you. Do not worry for me, Our Lady is with me and you!"

While they were pushing him into a car, he raised his handcuffed arms upwards and waved to the people who were helplessly looking on while he was being taken away. For days the secret agents had tried to force him to admit that the children were just poor misled hallucinating kids while they admonished him to stop celebrating evening Mass. He had refused to do either and now, here he was, handcuffed and forced to leave his church and village.

The police searched the church and found candles with a three-color flag, the flag of the Republic of Croatia without the socialist arms. These candles were brought by pilgrims from a shrine near Zagreb where such candles were sold openly in public. However in Hercegovina, such things were forbidden and so these candles were considered proof that the friars were up to something. This gave the police the excuse to close down the church by nailing two planks across the entrance. The parish house was also searched and turned upside down. A policewoman ordered some nuns to take off all their clothes and, after humiliating them, locked them up in a small room with nothing to eat or drink for twenty-four hours. The chaplain too was searched as if he were a criminal.

They threw books and magazines into the yard from the windows. They made lists of what they found as they believed it would be of help in pressing charges. They confiscated a considerable sum of money that pilgrims had given for Holy Masses. A receipt was given to Father Zrinko. It is said that those who took the money away had no peace of mind, they had nightmares so eventually they gave back the money.

That very day the visionaries had gone together to visit the parish of Čapljina in order to avoid meeting up with all the people and the police. When they came back, at about five o'clock in the afternoon, they met the police who stopped them for a police check at the entrance of their village. None of them had any ID cards on them. Luckily, a woman who was passing by confirmed that they were from the village so they were able to go home. When they arrived near the church they realized that it had been boarded up so they entered from behind through a little door in the sacristy. They hid in the room next to the altar and started praying.

Like every evening, my grandaunt Anica and some of her neighbours walked towards the church. There was nobody on the road. About hundred meters from the parish house a soldier was sitting, reading a newspaper. When the women approached, he jumped up, pointed his gun at them and ordered:

"Halt! Where are you going?"

"To the church!"

"You can't, go back to your homes!"

Anica looked at him in surprise undecided what to do. The soldier sat down and started reading his newspaper again. She knelt in front of him and started reciting her rosary. He shouted at her to go away but she calmly replied:

"If you can read your newspaper I too can pray here!"

The soldier was so astonished, he took out his mobile phone and called his superior:

"There is an old woman kneeling and praying, what should I do with her?"

The soldier was surprised at his commander's reply to let her go. From other directions, people were arriving for evening Mass. The police, on the bridge, would allow no one to pass. More and more people were gathering in front of the bridge and since they could not proceed, they sat on the ground by the road. Many of them took their rosaries and started praying. There was Friar Ivica Vego, too. When the time for Mass came, he said, loudly and decisively:

"We'll celebrate the Mass here, on the road!"

The police unexpectedly let the people pass. People were very excited and they ran towards the church, broke the planks and entered the church.

The Holy Mass was celebrated by the Capuchin monk Stanko Dodig, who had come from Rijeka to spend his vacation in his hometown. Father Stanko Vasilj, who used to play the organ, had been taken away for questioning along with two other friars. Father Zrinko and the nuns were still locked in the parish house, they were not allowed to go to church. While the visionaries were experiencing the apparition near the altar, those who were outside the church saw a great light come down onto the church. The Mass was ending when Father Zrinko was released from the parish house.

He ran into the church immediately, went to the altar and said in a shaky voice that it was the saddest day in his life because they had imprisoned Father Jozo. He was not able to talk any further because he started crying. The entire congregation cried with him.

Some of the people protested loudly. So in order to calm down the people, Father Zrinko called young Jakov to say what Our Lady had said during the apparition. He lifted the boy so everybody could see him while he was talking:

"Our Lady told us not to be afraid. She desires us to be full of joy and that joy should show in our faces. She will protect Father Jozo!"

These words were sufficient to calm down the people. They left the church silently and peacefully and everybody went home. There was a special atmosphere in the village that night: none of the children laughing or crying. Through the open windows you could hear the prayers being recited and the sobbing of the women. Many spent the night praying to God for their Parish Priest to be released.

The next morning Father Zrinko was summoned to the school for questioning. The agents of the secret police tried to intimidate him and convince him not to celebrate the evening Mass because according to them it was not in compliance with the Christian tradition and that the morning Mass would be sufficient as it had been in the past. The chaplain did not allow them to confuse him, he replied:

"Mass is not in memory of Jesus' last breakfast but in memory of his Last Supper!"

Hearing this, the president of Commission for religion smiled in embarrassment and let the friar go.

Some other men from the village were brought in and they were asked to testify against Father Jozo. One of them, a relation of mine, Peško, told them that not only would he not testify against the Parish Priest but he would be prepared to share any punishment with him. He felt extremely rebellious against this form of persecution and communist harassment of innocent people. He used to love saying that the devil himself could learn a lot from the communists.

The place of the first apparition (year 1981)

From the top: Filip, Zlata, Iva, Marija, Jakov, Vicka and Ivanka (year 1982)

*The painting of
naive painter
Vlado Falak*

The Conversion to the Living God

The next day after Father Jozo has been taken away, Father Tomislav Vlašić from Čapljina arrived to provide help for everyone. The same age as Jozo, he was a pedagogue and charismatic person, strong in faith with great experience in pastoral work and spiritual exercises. Father Tomislav was happy at the opportunity to work where such extraordinary events took place. He had an open-mind towards the apparitions. He felt that the situation should be closely observed, contemplated with care, together with deep prayer in order to come to the truth. He knew that not even the greatest Catholic theologians or philoshopers were able to penetrate God's secrets.

Father Tomislav had been at Medjugorje two days when Vicka and Jakov made their way to the altar to communicate the following message from Our Lady:

"A permanent sign will not appear so soon because there are still many who do not belive. Do not worry about Father Jozo because I will protect him."

Two Swiss reporters who had always followed the events in communist countries closely heard that a friar had been arrested and published this news all over Europe, and naturally from there it spread further around the world. Pilgrims continued arriving unworried by these facts. There were five young men who came on foot from Slovenia; a father with two daughters came from Macedonia and a group of Orthodox people arrived from Serbia. Croatian workers from America, Canada and Switzerland started to make pilgrimages.

That August evening 1981 many could not enter the church so they filled the nearby fields in throngs. Only a few were hosted by the families of Medjugorje, others slept as they could in cars or in fields under a starlight sky!

A different friar celebrated Mass every day each one seemingly inspired. For example, Father Ivan Dugandžić, preached about Jesus's love: "Forgive them Father, for they know not what are they doing!" The next evening, Father Tomislav repeated in a calm tone the words of Jesus: "Those who deny me I too will deny them before the Father."

Father Tomislav had assumed the role of mediator between the visionaries and the pilgrims. In that way he protected the chaplain, Father Zrinko, from attacks. He was cautious but firm in his attitude and this seemed to keep his interlocutors at a distance; his face expressed great spirituality and he commanded respect at the very first contact because of his serious and perhaps "distant" look.

Even the secret police recognized his authority and so they avoided direct confrontation with him. Therefore he was the most suitable person for being with the parishioners in those hard times.

Father Tomislav gave courage to the inhabitants of Medjugorje and taught them that the Revelations speak of a living God, who is much more than a good Father who cares for His children. This is what the Church believes and therefore it generally accepts the possibility of apparitions, which repropose everything that God has revealed to Man throughout history. The central biblical theme is the conversion to the living God, and it is followed by penance and prayer. Jesus sent his apostles to announce the conversion of all peoples. The Church continues it. This is why Our Lady's messages are centred on conversion, prayer, penance, the Holy Mass ... messages that the visionaries repeat untiringly.

Father Tomislav said that the Comunists accused Father Jozo of being the cause of all these events, but he himself considered it very unlikely because none of the visionaries was a member of Jozo's prayer group. In fact he hardly knew the children. As for him, Father Tomislav let it be known that he believed that the apparitions were authentic, regardless of the great difficulties due to the visionaries themselves, who had a limited vocabulary and it was very hard for them to describe something that was so great. For this reason, he encouraged the inhabitants of Medjugorje and the pilgrims to pray and fast as Our Lady requested, because God knows better than anyone what His plan is here. Everyday he diligently updated the Parish Chronicle regarding the visionaries' reports on their meetings with the Blessed Virgin Mary.

The Communist Authorities had hoped that everything would stop after imprisoning padre Jozo and they showed even more ruthlessness in harassing people. They went from village to village, summoned people to meetings and "advised" them from going to Medjugorje. They were particularily menacing towards young people, threatening to refuse them work permits and to throw them in jail if they should go to the apparitions. In fact, some were frightened and stopped coming to Medjugorje, while the others went by hidden paths in order to avoid the police. In spite of everything, there was always a great number of people attending the Holy Mass every evening.

The more the people felt free to declare their faith, the more the police threatened the visionaries and their relations. Mirjana's father took her to Sarajevo for a week, in the hope of protecting her. She consoled herself with the idea that she was near enough to return to Medjugorje for the weekends. Ivanka too returned to Mostar. Both visionaries had to present themselves to the police daily. Once a police officer was following Mirjana and he observed her while she had a vision. The girl seemed to be out of time and space. The police officer was so impressed he decided to stop following her. In fact Mirjana said that the police in Sarajevo were not so rude and violent as in Čitluk; they only smiled ironically when she told them that she had visions every day.

The Queen of Peace

Towards the end of August Father Zrno arrived from the United States to celebrate 50 years of priesthood. He wanted to know from the visionaries if the Holy Mother had indicated a particular name for herself in Medjugorje. The children asked Her and the reply was:

"I am the Queen of Peace!"

One evening Marija entered her bedroom and saw Our Lady waiting for her by the window. Marija called Vicka who was nearby. Our Lady asked them if they wanted to enter a convent explaining that it was not an obligation but She would have been happy if they made that choice. She advised them to think carefully about it before making any decision. A few evenings later the visionaries asked Our Lady:

"Dear Lady, what should we do?"

"Dedicate your life to God, my angels!"

They realized that they had to make a decision on their own because they were absolutely free to make their own decisions.

Ivan immediately decided to become a monk choosing the Franciscan monastery in Visoko near Sarajevo.

Vicka and Marija considered becoming nuns. Jakov was too young to make any decision because he had to complete his primary education. Mirjana and Ivanka talked about their future at home, too. Mirjana's grandmother listened to them and said:

"I am really surprised that Our Lady appears to you both, considering that you talk to boys!"

Mirjana replied calmly:

"Dear grandmother, Our Lady did not come to make monsters of us!"

In the meantime Jakov's father arrived in Medjugorje from Sarajevo. He was reserved and neutral in his attitude, he neither encouraged nor discouraged his son. Mirjana's father arrived too and, in tears, he begged Father Vlašić to advise his daughter to leave Medjugorje, to return home and continue her education. He then discovered that the headmaster of the High School had suspended her because he was afraid that Mirjana would talk about her visions to other students. Her father arranged for her to attend another school. The many people, of various faith, that visited Mirjana's house all experienced beautiful "inner views".

The visionary herself was happy because she had more time to be with Our Lady and ask Her questions about Her life of which the Bible speaks so little.

Ivan arrived at the seminary of Visoko in Bosnia on 28th August. The very same evening he had a vision of the Holy Mother who told him to rest and not to worry.

During this period when the visionaries were forced to separate, Father Stanko Vasilj, a writer, poet and composer, who had very much suffered in the communist prisons, feeling sadness for Father Jozo and inspired by Heaven, wrote and composed the following hymn of Medjugorje:

We come to You, Dear Mother,
from all parts of the World,
we bring You our problems
and with them our desires.

Ref: Look on us, console us,
lay your hands upon us;
intercede for us to Your Son.
Mother of Peace, pray for us.

The whole Church looks to You
the last star of salvation;
purify us, embrace us,
with all our hearts we pray You

Your little Bijakovo
and all Medjugorje
together spread Your glory
and exalt Your name.

For all the love dear Mother
You have poured out to us here,
we promise You in future
to be better than we were.

(Words and music by Father Stanko Vasilj)

This beautiful song was heard for the first time on 30th August in the church of Medjugorje. Father Stanko played the organ. The song immediately entered the people's hearts, they learned it easily and it has since been sung whenever people have gathered together. It is interesting to note that, since the apparitions began, people started to sing only spiritual songs in honor of Our Lady on weddings and merry-makings while the other popular, traditional and freedom-loving songs were left out.

In the meantime, strange things happened in the Mostar prison. Guards locked Father Jozo's cell in the evening but they found it unlocked and wide open in the morning. There was a bright light in his cell by night although there was no bulb in there to light it up. When the prison guards reported these strange goings-on their officers got angry at such "fanaticism" and locked-up the guards with the friar. Two high-ranking officials were called to check the matter personally to verify exactly what was happening. Jozo's

*Father Stanko and
the parish choir*

cell was locked in front of them but later it was found unlocked. The high officials also saw the light which seemed to come from nowhere; this obviously disturbed them. It is said that some of the guards converted.

On Sunday 30th August, Vicka, Marija and Jakov had a vision in Marinko Ivanković's house. They prayed and sang. Our Lady appeared among them and greeted them with: "Praised be Jesus!" Vicka asked Her if it was true that Father Jozo's cell was locked in the evening and found unlocked in the morning.

"Yes, it is true but no one believes it."

Ivanka asked how Mirjana was and Our Lady replied:

"Mirjana is sad because she is alone. I will show her to you." In that moment Our Lady showed to them, Mirjana in tears.

Vicka asked advice for a woman who wanted to leave her husband because he illtreated her.

"Let her remain close to him and accept her suffering. Jesus, Himself, also suffered."

"Dear Lady, which is the best form of fasting?"

"Bread and water."

Bishop Žanić was very brave, he wrote a letter of protest to Sergej Krajger, the Yugoslav president, (a Slovenian who was Tito's first heir) asking for the immediate release of the friar, who was unjustly accused. Among other things, he wrote: "...As a Catholic bishop and person in charge of the diocese of Mostar, I deny all the slander and unfair accusations against my priests. Such irresponsible behaviour by no means helps to judge the events in Medjugorje objectively. Such offensive actions offend all fundamental human rights."

A copy of the letter was sent to all the competent governing bodies, the Episcopal Conference of Yugoslavia, the Holy Seat in Rome and the entire Catholic Press in the country. The inhabitants of Medjugorje learned about the Bishop's letter when Father Tomislav read it after Mass. Everybody hoped that Father Jozo would be released as a consequence.

They say that a young man from Belgrade, son of a colonel, who was baptized according to the eastern rite as a child and who was brought up in the atheistic ideology came to Medjugorje to climb the Apparition Hill. As soon as he came to the place where the children had seen the Virgin Mary, for the first time two soldiers appeared and beat him so cruelly that he could barely crawl back to the village. He told the people who aided him afterwards that the two soldiers had no idea who he was ... but ... they would both be in deep trouble when they found out.

So it was ... a few days later the soldiers "disappeared" from the village and were never seen again.

Early September, Vicka went to Mostar to sit for her mathematics exam. A professor stopped her at the school entrance and told her to remove her necklace with a chain and cross, otherwise he would not let her in. He also mocked her by saying:

"You were in the newspapers, you don't have to sit for your exam, you passed yours with your Virgin Mary!"

Vicka did not reply. She turned on her heels, she went straight to the school office, collected her documents together and returned home. After several days she received a notice advising her that she had passed the exam, although she did not sit for it and that she was allowed to continue her education. Vicka left the school. She stayed in Medjugorje so that she should keep Jakov company. And that was Our Lady's wish, too.

The school year began and the children from villages around Medjugorje were continually being harassed. The teachers made them remove any crosses from their necklaces, forbade them to speak about the visions, acted roughly, gave them lower marks than they deserved. The children did not react in any way to such provocations neither at Čitluk nor at Mostar: they were very reserved, well-mannered and disciplined so that these provocations were a total failure and soon ceased.

Mirjana still had visions in her living-room. Paša, a Muslim who was sick, was present at one of these apparitions, and she said she too saw Our Lady. Mirjana asked Our Lady if this were true and She confirmed and praised the girl saying her devotion was an example to others.

During the first days of school, a girl wanted to make friends with Mirjana so she invited her to go out together one evening but the visionary did not want to. During the next apparition, Our Lady advised Mirjana to stop associating with that girl as her intention was to drug Mirjana.

At the beginning of school year, Marija went to Mostar to continue her education. She lived with her relatives and went to school there. She attended the Holy Mass every evening and she experienced a vision in the church. One Saturday she was going back home to Medjugorje by bus. There were many pilgrims in the bus heading for Medjugorje. She hid behind her friends so as not to be recognized and whispered: "Please, just listen to what they are saying about the apparitions ... none of us would ever dream of saying such things!"

Ivanka returned home to Mostar where she often experienced visions, but she lived withdrawn and very few people knew about her. She could not wait for Christmas when her father would be back from Germany on holiday for he would surely provide her with the protection she so badly desired. Little Jakov continued school unwillingly and went around telling everyone that he didn't need to go to school. The Virgin Mary was more than enough for him. During one of the apparitions Our Lady told Jakov to love his class-mates. Like a typical child he replied hastily:

"But they are so boring!"

"Accept them as your penance."

"Very well, I will dear Lady, but please don't tell my mother!"

Our Lady called Mirjana to Medjugorje for a short period to convince her little, playful cousin to continue attending school. Vicka was in Medjugorje, but she just did not have the time to look after Jakov. When she came home, tired and sweaty from the hard work in the fields, she used to find her yard full of people waiting for her. She could not count on Jakov, he would disappear. However, with a radiant smile on her face, she received the people as if they were her dearest relatives. Vicka forgot even to eat when she had to speak to them:

"Don't ever forget that God is our Father and that he sent us Our Mother to convert us. If you only knew how much She loves us. Ask Her for help whenever you need to, She will help you, She will recommend you to Her Son. Pray frequently, Our Lady says that prayer is our most powerful weapon. Fast, satan is afraid of a fast."

She would go to church with Jakov in the evening. After the rosary, the vision and the Holy Mass they would pray for the sick. Vicka was untiring in praying for the sick. She frequently used to put her hands on the heads of people. All these experiences made a new person of her: before she was so timid and did not dare go out of the house after sunset. Now she dared go to the Podbrdo Hill by herself, in the middle of the night to pray to Our Lady.

On the Feast of the Birth of the Blessed Virgin Mary, Jakov and Vicka had their daily vision. Little Jakov gave his hand to Our Lady and said: "Our Lady, happy birthday to You!" Vicka did not dare do the same. Our Lady took Jakov's hand and smiled.

In that period the little boy was very worried about his favorite football team Dinamo. He asked Our Lady if the team would win the football league. She smiled at him warmly and thus showed how a real mother understands everything.

After only one week of school Ivanka returned to Medjugorje on Saturday afternoon. She looked for Marija and her mother Iva told her she was probably on the hill in some secret place with the others. So Ivanka went away to look for them. Soon after Iva left the house too and not far away, under an oak tree, she found Ivanka crying. She asked her what was the matter. Ivanka replied that Our Lady had appeared and she had seen her mother with Her again. She explained that every-time she saw her mum she wanted to cry. She wanted her mother to be with her now. Iva hugged her and said: "Dear child, I understand because a mother is always a mother!"

The next day, on Sunday, Ivanka, Vicka, Marija and Jakov had an apparition. The little boy kept questioning Our Lady:

"Dear Lady, do You appear to Ivan in the seminary?"

"Yes, just like I do to you."

"Dear Lady, will You help us to study?"

"God's help manifests itself everywhere."

Ivanka asked Her again for a sign:

"Be patient, my angels!"

Vicka asked why a young boy had killed himself. The reply was:

"Satan took hold of him. This young man should not have done it. The devil tries to dominate people. He takes everything into his hands, but the force of God is more powerful, and God will overcome."

Jakov asked if there would be a Mass on mount Križevac for the Feast of the Exaltation of the Cross.

"Yes my angels." She answered.

"Will the police surround the church?"

"Nothing like that. People should pray and stay in church as long as possible. Go in Peace!"

After this vision, as many time before, Our Lady left the symbols: the cross, the heart and the sun behind Her.

Ivan too, although being away from his home, was praying and preparing for the Feast of the Exaltation of the Holy Cross. While he was praying in the seminary chapel, a bright light with Our Lady in the midst of it suddenly appeared. She told him:

"Pray very much especially on Sunday, so that the great sign, the gift of God may come. Pray incessantly, with fervour, so that God may have mercy on His children. Go in peace, my angel. May the blessing of God accompany you. Amen. Good-bye."

While the apparitions continued and occurred wherever the visionaries found themselves, Father Jozo was suffering atrociously in jail. Ruthless inquisitors wanted to make him give in ... force him to confess that he and seven hundred dissidents, who lived in Germany, had been plotting a counter-revolution in Yugoslavia.

Parishioner Mladen Bulić, who was in the Mostar hospital, was a witness to his sufferings.

He saw Father Jozo dragged between two policemen, he could hardly walk. When Mladen asked the friar how he was, Father Jozo replied: "As you see!"

Mladen realized some of his teeth were missing and his right cheek was all swollen. He had been brutally beaten-up, in a tired whisper the friar asked:

"How are things in Medjugorje?"

One of the policeman interrupted:

"What are you worrying about? Tonight we're going to slit your throat!"

Mladen protested: "You can't do that to him! You've already beaten him up but you can't kill him!"

Father Jozo indicated, with a movement of his head, that it was better to be quiet because he, Jozo, would pay dearly for any form of help, even expressed only in words.

MEDJUGORJE:
a Gift for the World

Father Jozo's destiny caused world-wide interest among newspaper reporters who flocked, one after the other, to Medjugorje. At the end of the summer 1981, I was at home in Italy where I had been living for fifteen years. I knew nothing of the apparitions until I read an article regarding these events in an Italian magazine. There was a picture of the six visionaries and while I was looking at it I felt immensely happy. I believed in those children from my father's hometown. I really believed they had actually seen the Virgin Mary.

That very same moment I wanted to go there but it was impossible as my mother-in-law, who lived with us, was very ill. I was afraid to call my relatives in Medjugorje because I knew their phone was tapped and I certainly did not want to cause them any more trouble other than they already had! I was very cautious when I called my father in Opatija because very probably his phone was tapped, too. My dad told me:

"I do not know the children, but I do know their grandparents, they have always been god-fearing people and very honest. I do not believe that their grandchildren are liars. Life is very hard for everybody in Medjugorje now, some are in prison, the others are harassed and persecuted, but Our Lady is with them and everything will be all right.

The other day Mijo Buntić, whom you visited in Čitluk on business, told me that something is really happening down there, something that cannot be man's deeds. The police took his car number, but he did not care: he went to church where he sang and prayed with all the people and he said the singing was like one single voice. According to him our people are literally reborn and have never shown such goodness and caring."

From that very moment I started reading the Italian Catholic press more carefully and discovered that a petition in favour of Father Jozo, demanding his release, was being organized by the Italian Catholics. They were insisting that the Vatican and the Government should use their influence to get Friar Jozo freed.

In a short time, the Yugoslav president received twenty thousand letters soliciting for Father Jozo.

That summer of 1981 there were two Italians, Rita and Pietro, on holiday on the island of Korčula in Croazia. They met an old priest there, who, in a mixture of Italian and Latin, told them about the apparitions of Our Lady in Hercegovina. His eyes were full of tears as he told them: "Please, go there for me, if you can, I am too old for travelling and only God knows what I 'd give to be able to go!"

They replied that they would go there to please the priest and so they set off for Mostar. When they were near Ljubuški they asked where Medjugorje was but nobody wanted to tell them. When they arrived at Čitluk they were very surprised that nobody wanted to help them find "the village of the apparitions". What they did not realise was that the people were afraid they might be communist spies, also the two Italian tourists were unaware that access to the "hill of apparitions" was forbidden. But, they were firm in their intention, they did not want to give up. They noticed a group of people who were travelling on foot, they followed them and so at last they found themselves in front of the Medjugorje church.

On entering it was clear from the smell of sweat that the people had arrived directly from their work in the fields. In front of the church were piles of rakes and hoes.

Rita and Pietro pushed their way to the altar and saw the friar and the children kneeling and saying the rosary. Although

142

they were praying in Croatian, they joined in the prayer as if it had been in their own language. They saw the children stand up and go into a room to the right of the altar. There was complete silence in the church and they felt immense bliss and peace in their hearts. The Holy Mass followed and then the prayer for healing. They stayed in church for more than three hours, forget-ting the sweaty smelling air, and they experienced great joy together. They felt as if they were reborn and "one" along with those humble people around them.

They needed to meet the friar: they approached him and, miraculously, he spoke their language. It was Father Tomislav who explained exactly what was happening there. He told them of Our Lady's messages and they explained how they had arrived here in order to please a priest from Korčula. The friar smiled mysteriously and said:

"You confirm what I realized as soon as I came to this parish. Nobody comes here by chance. Those who come are expressly invited. You did not come to please that priest but to please Our Lady. She called you just as She calls Her children, one by one, and asks us to accept and live by Her messages. You will witness that the Holy Mother wishes to lead us all to God and to do this, She needs us all and our prayers. Before all this happened I was a hypocrite because I imagined I didn't need any messages of the Virgin Mary. Now that I feel what words cannot describe I am ready to dedicate myself completely to Our Holy Mother and I shall pray according to Her indications with even more devotion than ever before.

Now I realise that before, even though I was a man of God, I was too busy doing things which I believed were my duty to do. Here in Medjugorje I, too, am learning with the pilgrims that it is of the utmost importance that man surrenders to God completely, only then will he have time enough."

The Feast of the Exaltation of the Cross

On 14th September during the Feast of the Exaltation of the cross the army allowed the people to climb Mount Križevac ... just as the Holy Mother had announced ... on the condition that they did not stop there longer than 4 p.m. It was a bright, sunny day with a light breeze just, perfect for the climb of the multitude who arrived that day from all around ... and further! All of them had come to take part in the Holy Mass. With a microphone in his hand Father Tomislav commented the mysteries of the rosary while he climbed to the top of the Križevac. At his rear thousands of youngsters followed, some bare-footed.

After the sermon, which touched the hearts of all those present, Father Stanko Vasilj started to sing an old and very touching hymn: "We greet you Holy Body of Jesus, sacrificed for us." The song spread in waves, embracing everyone there ... and there were thousands and thousands of people.

At the end of the Mass the priest blessed everyone ... near and far ...: "All of you here now ... all of you in your homes ... all of you in our country ... all of you working abroad in the rich country of the U.S.A. ... distant Australia ... hot Africa ... all who are sick ... the aged ... your children ... your suffering ... all your prayers, all your bare feet and all your sweating and fatigue ... The Almighty God, the Father the Son and the Holy Spirit blesses all and everything!"

Joy filled everyone as they burst into merrymaking and singing on the top of the hill while they waited for the people at the bottom of the hill to move away ... so that they could then descend.

A man from Osijek said that he had been so touched by the sermon that he would come again the next year, too. A student from Zagreb said that he experienced the sermon as God's call, to all those people. An elderly man from the parish said that he was happy to see so many young people there, it was a sign that they had not forgotten God.

At 4 o'clock, just as the police had ordered, everybody left the hill peacefully. Many of them went to the church to attend the pilgrims' Mass. Stipe Ćavar, the author of the book "The first months of the apparitions in Medjugorje", was present, too.

He remembers two women from Split who said that they were late because the police had almost prevented them from coming to Križevac. On their way back, they asked for some water in the Vasilj-Grlić house. The master of the house offered them something to eat and drink. He said: "We are off to church but you drink and eat as you please. Have a rest and when you've finished just close the front door and come to Mass too.' Both women were most surprised at his great hospitality.

The visionaries continued to experience the apparitions every evening, Our Lady comforted them and told them not to worry about Father Jozo who would endure everything because She was protecting him. She showed them Father Jozo in his cell and they prayed together for him. The children too were willing to go to prison for him if necessary, and they were still not afraid even after another two friars were imprisoned and falsely accused.

Nobody in the parish could understand why the friar had been imprisoned. Several agents had accused him referring to what he had said during his sermon on 11th July:

"He came to free me a slave, you a slave, who have lived in slavery for forty years…"

The secret police imagined that the forty years of slavery alluded to the fortieth anniversary of the people's insurrection against fascism. So, having twisted the words to interprete them as it suited them best, they used false witnesses, to swear that the priest had encouraged the people to rebellion and this was enough to imprison him.

Milan Vuković, an expert lawyer, came from Zagreb to defend Father Jozo. He convinced the Court of Mostar to observe the correct legal procedure and he called three-hundred-thirty witnesses for the defense. The parishioners gladly agreed to be witnesses even if this might have meant trouble for them with the authorities. During a two-day preliminary debate, the lawyer did his best to explain that the words in the sermon referred to the Gospel by Luke 4, 18-19 and to the prophet Isaiah's statement 16, 1-2. He added that the number "forty" was symbolic and that every priest recited from the breviary: "…for forty years you have bothered this generation!…'"

The District Attorney aimed to make the defense attorney look ridiculous by saying:

"We too have read the Gospel a little!"

The defense attorney Vuković responded quickly:

"That is why we are here, if you had read it properly there would have been no trial at all!"

Lawyer Vuković did everything possible to have the friar freed; his efforts towards revealing the truth were also endangering himself. This was confirmed by the letter that his wife, who was also a lawyer, had put into his bag before he left Zagreb: "Dear Milan, farewell! Don't forget that you have two childern who will still need you for a long time......"

Witnesses claimed that one of the judges (from Montenegro), refused to sentence Zovko because he considered him innocent.

The investigation was difficult and hard for the inhabitants of Medjugorje, but they gritted their teeth and withstood it. Instead of protesting they recited more rosaries and fasted. The visionaries prayed with Our Lady and She comforted them and encouraged them not to give up, as everything would turn out well in the end.

After the evening Mass in Medjugorje, the people formed a procession on their way home to the nearby villages. They went towards Bijakovići, Šurmanci, Miletina, - passing by the Križevac, going on foot across Tromedja to Čitluk and farther still. Merry pilgrims' songs could be heard everywhere: "We have come to You, dear Mother", "There is a long path to Heaven", "How beautiful You are, Virgin Mary!".

At the end of September, a great flame appeared on the Apparition Hill. The hill could be seen burning from quite a distance. The guards watching the hill saw the flame and were surprised there was a flame, a fire, but nothing was burning...there was no smoke!... On Sunday, the day after this strange fire, little Jakov said that Our Lady would appear to the people at midday and everybody would see Her.

Everyone rushed towards the Apparition Hill, ignoring the guards who in vain tried to stop them. Many claimed that they saw the Queen of Peace at the place of the apparitions that day.

A Jesuit, Tommaso Beck, head of a House of Spiritual Exercises in Milan, arrived incognito a little after the strange "fire" had occurred on the Apparition Hill.

He was very impressed by the peoples' devotion ... devotion that he had not experienced either at Lourdes or Fatima. He believed that it was important that most things had happened in the church and that the people were not influenced emotionally by happenings on the Apparition Hill.

Father Beck noticed how the visionaries prayed in front of the altar, how the congregation listened to the Gospel and attended the sacrament of Holy Communion. He considered that it was a good thing that the emotion of the moment when Mother Mary appeared turned into careful attention to the word of God in the presence of the priests. Father Beck was very impressed with the visionaries too. He realized that they were quite normal children, far from being fanatical, who relayed the Holy Messages as accurately as possible.

On returning to Italy, Father Beck declared that the apparitions of Medjugorje were important for the entire Church and that their spiritual guide, Father Vlašić, was in fact guiding the visionaries in the best possible way, helping them to grow and to live the messages they were relaying to others.

On the last day of September Vicka and Jakov went to a nearby village called Šurmanci to pray with a young girl who had cancer. The Madonna had said that she would be with Her, in Heaven, the next day ... And so it was. The girl passed away during the night after praying with the two children. Her family dressed her in white just as Our Lady had recommended.

148

My cousin's wife bore a son at the end of October. Her husband Ante was supposed to go to the Apparition Hill to keep watch on the day that she was dismissed from the hospital. As he wanted to spend that first evening at home with his wife and baby, he asked a friend to substitute him. The friend agreed so my cousin went to the guards' co-ordinator to ask for his permission to go home. The man shouted at him and told him that he had to go on guard and that he would accept no excuses.

Ante returned to his wife feeling resigned and frustrated and told her: "Don't be surprised if the police arrive shortly to take me away." Half an hour later a policeman, who was their acquaintance, did arrive. The officer was obviously embarrassed while he congratulated Ante on the arrival of his son, he told him he had orders to take him to the police station in Čitluk. Luckily at Čitluk there was a more humane and kinder officer who told him: "Go back to your son and wife and don't worry, I will find an excuse to let you off this duty!"

Father Jozo's upcoming trial was in the minds of everyone including the visionaries. They insisted there would be a permanent sign which would "soften" the authorities. Regarding this is the following answer:

"I promised to give you a sign, I will fulfill my promise, and you must pray, pray, pray and believe firmly. If these people do not convert it will be very serious for them. Do not ask me about things which are not important or things out of curiosity. The most important thing is prayer, my angels."

The trial started on 22nd October, 1981. Friar Jozo sat on the bench, his hands handcuffed as if he were a ferocious criminal. In spite of his utmost efforts, his lawyer was unable to prove the priest's innocence to those who absolutely did not want to even consider it! The Friar was sentenced to three and a half years hard labour in the notorious jail of Foča in Bosnia. He was locked in cell number sixteen where there were eighty prisoners.

Their narrow beds were piled one above the other. There was no heating and they had no blankets either to protect them from the bitter cold. The food was very bad and scarce, so they all went hungry.

Conditions were awful with just three toilets and one shower for all these men, so the prisoners were full of fleas and lice. During the day they worked in work shops making furniture. Father Jozo soon fell ill because when he arrived from the Mostar prison he was already exhausted and breathing with difficulty. Now he became worried, not so much about his physical state, but for his mental and psychic condition. It was hard for him to be imprisoned without being able to prove his innocence.

When he dared protest to the guards because they did not allow him to have the Bible and the Gospel with him, which was against the Geneva Convention, they beat, slapped and maltreated him, both physically and psychically. His lawyer also protested and declared that in the Kingdom of Yugoslavia prisoners condemned of communism were allowed to read Marx's The Capital, while here they did not allow a priest to have the New Testament.

In spite of everything, Father Jozo did not give in: he prayed devotedly for all those who had convicted him unjustly, for the guards and the most violent of the prisoners who became his friends. Luckily, the friar found an Italian grammar book in the prison library and started to learn Italian.

While he was in prison, his substitute Father Zrinko was having more and more to do in the parish. To overcome his worry and sorrow over Father Jozo's situation, he took care of the fruit-trees in the garden, which helped him together with prayers, and he did his best to re-assure and encourage everyone and himself too. Father Tomislav was a great help as he had even psycho-analyzed the carriers of Our Lady messages and had made a statement accordingly:

"Because of the circumstances these child visionaries have to tell about their experiences, time after time. They are continually besieged by the pilgrims with superficial questions which they answer simply and as briefly as possible. One of the priests has said: "No matter how much I would like to see Our Blessed Lady, I could never stand the stress and all the questions Vicka manages to put up with!" The children lack theological expression which would of course satisfy theology. As the Bible confirms there are some people and institutions who are very narrow minded towards divine messages. Psychology teaches us of the inner resistance that man suffers when he does not want to change... even if it means his healing or only his intimate, moral and spiritual healing. The path is long, sometimes it takes years before a person accepts, and gathers the fruits of salvation. We experience this ourselves. The most difficult step is that of one's conversion.

Our psychological structure is sometimes very rigid or we have attitudes and opinions that crystalize not only our positive acquisitions but also those negative tendencies which have taken root in us. Such difficulties are not only experienced by the visionaries alone but are also shared by us too. This prevents us from renewing our faith despite God's help.

I believe that we will be able to understand the importance of the apparitions only when we allow an inner change to take place in ourselves. While we retain rigid attitudes, even though we believe they are justified, while we allow ourselves to be distracted by external facts: which priests work in Medjugorje? .. and how? their methods, the way they are, or inner elements (not being prepared for who are the people of Hercegovina?) ... or .. perhaps inner resistence like refusing conversions ... or prayer ... or fasting ... not only will we not understand the real meaning of these mysterious apparitions but, perhaps, we will throw the stones of our own personal logic to challenge them! If on the contrary we were so inclined, then we could be preparing the way the right understanding to contemplate these mysterious happenings. This coincides with the ultimate goal of these apparitions: conversion to God. I personally consider that the apparitions in Medjugorje are authentic but ... it is my personal opinion and I do not wish to prejudice, in any way, the opinions of the Church, Keeper and Master of the Truth!"

A Glance beyond Life

One afternoon Vicka was visiting Jakov and together they were looking at some photographs received from some pilgrims. Jakov's mother was there too and, for a moment she went out of the room into the yard. When she returned the children were no longer there. Our Lady had appeared and had invited them to go with Her to Paradise. Little Jakov was afraid because he thought that he would leave forever and childishly said to Our Lady:

"Blessed Mother, take Vicka, they are eight brothers and sisters while I am an only child. What would my mother do without me?"

Our Lady smiled, gently took his hand and the wall opened in front of them. They started to go up while Jakov's house and Medjugorje got farther and farther away in the distance below them. Vicka later confided that she had seen a man standing at the entrance of Paradise; that all the people in Paradise had been young and were dressed in pink, yellow and grey. They were neither fat nor thin, everybody was happily talking and singing together and angels were flying above them. After that Our Lady took them to Purgatory there they saw no one, they only felt their, presence and suffering. Jakov said he saw something moving in the grey mist and when they arrived at the doors of Hell he - closed his eyes because it was so horrible he did not want to see it. Vicka instead saw everything that was happening.

Later she described how a great fire was burning and how devils were pushing people into it and, when they emerged, how they were transformed into dreadful creatures. Both children heard frightful lamenting ... desperate crying and ferocious cursing and swearing. It was obvious that everyone hated each other in this Hell and, in that very moment, Jakov's mother saw them in the room again and there they were as if nothing had happened!

Every evening after the Holy Mass for the poor and sick celebrated by Father Tomislav, the congregation would bring sick people's clothes for the blessing. Jure Bošnjak's relatives did the same because he was paralyzed and hospitalized in Mostar. When he then wore these clothes that had been

Author's daughter Lara and son Janko thread the tobacco leaves with cousin Silvana and friend Umberto

blessed he made a complete recovery to the great surprise of the doctors! A certain Slavko, suffering from spinal disease, was suddenly cured during one of these Masses and also Fila Kozina who suffered severe migranes alleged that she too had been cured! She had prayed and fasted for her recovery. Nada Bagarić, who suffered from muscular dystrophy, arrived from Germany and recovered while she was praying in the church. Olga Rulović, a Russian paralytic from Monte Negro, also declared her own miraculous recovery: of how she returned home healthy and well.

It is not noted however, just how many pilgrims experienced "inner healing" but the priests reported that they had never seen so many people confessing and converting!

Sometimes Our Lady would tell the children that She was pleased that so many people had answered Her calls but that there were still a great many who had not converted and for whom they had to pray and fast. She spoke about the value of the Holy Mass, but She also added that it was better not to attend the Mass at all than to attend unprepared.

In early November, without any "ado" or announcement, a world famous healer and leader of the renewal of the charismatic movement in Italy, Father Robert Faricy, arrived in Medjugorje. Father Faricy is a Jesuit and professor of spirituality at the Papal University in Rome. He had read that Our Lady was appearing in Yugoslavia and he immediately travelled to Split where he knew a priest, who was willing to accompany and lead him to Medjugorje. When they arrived at the parish house, one of the friars looked at Faricy suspiciously and asked him why he had come. At that very moment Father Tomislav entered the rectory and recognized Father Faricy. They had met in Rome six months before during a convention of the Charismatics.

Later, in his booklet, Father Faricy wrote that Father Tomislav followed Our Lady's messages carefully, precisely and, being full of understanding, strength and humanity, was a safe guide and comfort to the visionaries. As for the visionaries themselves he remarked that they were quite normal individuals and hardly different from the other children of their own age. Of himself, he confided that during that first visit to Medjugorje he felt very close to Our Lady, that now he was much more aware of Her maternal presence in his life. He declared that he had no doubts as to the authenticity of the apparitions because of the intense atmosphere of holiness, reverence and piety that he had felt in the congregation in church. He was convinced that Medjugorje would be no less important than Lourdes and Fatima and that it would become the greatest Marian sanctuary in spite of the powers of darkness that aimed to destroy it.

Preparation for a Happy Departure from this Life

One November night, during his sermon, Father Tomislav mentioned a parishioner whom he had visited to administer the last rites. He explained that he had entered the house saying:

"Praised be Jesus!".

"Praised be Jesus and welcome Father!" was the answer. "I know that I have cancer and in a few hours I must go to meet the Father. I have fulfilled my duties here. I have brought up my children in truth and the christian faith; they've had a good education. I have given everything to my wife and children and

I have observed the laws of God. My good friar, what I need now is a passport recommendation to Heaven..."

After telling this story, the priest asked all those who were present in church to ask themselves how they would react knowing that they had only one more hour to live. This helped everyone to understand why Our Lady's messages insist on prayer and reconciliation with God.

The visionary Mirjana also met a dying person. It was a young sister nun who Our Lady had said would soon join Her. After this apparition, Mirjana had to communicate this message to the sister who, to Mirjana's amazement, joyfully accepted the news.

Mirjana told her parents, friends and everybody who came to the apparitions that the Blessed Virgin Mary had told her that She, Mary, had been a normal and simple woman in Nazareth who had experienced poverty and had just as many problems as any other mortal. That is why we can address Her for all our needs in life even more than we do to our mother who brought us into the world. This is why Mirjana became closer and closer to the Holy Mother asking question after question about those things she yearned to know. For example:

"Our Lady, what quilt have those young people who have been brought up without any religion?"

'The young have minds to think and eyes to see. When they walk around the cities, they see churches or mosques; they should ask themselves what they are for!"

When Mirjana told this to a priest, he asked if Our Lady had really mentioned mosques and she confirmed it! As for the priests in general, during an apparition, Our Lady asked Mirjana to relay a message to those who disregard their faith because of the faults of some priests:

"You do not go to church because of a priest or to hear about his private life; you go to hear the word of God!"

Whenever possible, Mirjana explained to people just how important it is to pray for non-believers and for those who do not know of Christ. She used to repeat frequently:

"Please, answer Our Lady's call, pray for those who are far from God, who have never met Him or heard of Him. Every prayer for non-believers wipes a tear from Our Lady's face."

More than by words, Our Holy Mother taught Her chosen few through Her loving ways with them and Marija realized this when she said: "I feel that I must do my best to give to everyone at least a small part of the love I receive from Our Heavenly Mother".

There were written reports on the daily messages received by the visionaries in December 1981. I will quote only those that are perhaps of general importance.

On 7th December, Our Lady told the visionaries:

"It is true that people are converting, but all are not yet doing so."

The next day, on the Feast of the Immaculate Conception, the Holy Mother appeared to look very serious to the visionaries. She was kneeling and praying with Her arms spread out:

"My beloved Son, I beseech you to forgive the world its great sins that offend You!"

On 9th December, during the apparition, She prayed together with the visionaries saying:

"Oh! My Son Jesus, forgive these sins even if there are so many of them!"

Vicka and Jakov asked if it were true that the people saw Our Lady at the top of Križevac by the great cross. The answer was:

"Yes, I am there almost every day. I pray by the cross. My Son carried the cross. He suffered on the cross and thus He saved the world. Everyday I beseech my Son to forgive the sins of the world."

Frane Franić, at that time, the Archbishop of Split and President of Episcopal Conference of Yugoslavia, after hearing about the apparitions from the Jesuits Beck and Faricy, decided to go there and see for himself regardless of his high rank in the Church Hierarchy. Here is a part of his statement on this experience:

"I went to the sanctuary of Our Lady of Medjugorje privately, to pray. I arrived on 19th of December. The church was full of people and I sat in one of the central pews. I had a scarf around my neck to hide my ecclesiastical collar. There were many people around me particularly young people, and they all listened attentively to the sermon which was on faith and its miracles. It was clear that the priest firmly believed what he was saying. He was obviously not "contaminated" by the latest modern theology or impossible exegesis.

I was favourably-impressed but this is my private opinion and I will leave to the experts of the Church to make their judgment on the authenticity of these events."

Christmas 1981

It was Christmas time: time of reconciliation and joy bringing new hope to Friar Ivica Vego from Mostar. A few months before, he and another friar had been suspended 'a divinis' by the head of the Franciscan order for administering holy sacraments in Franciscan chapels to the people who did not want to go to their own parishes, which were led by the diocesan clergy. (According to the Pope's decree of 1975, Bishop Žanić decreed that eight major Franciscan parishes in Hercegovina were to be administred by the diocesan clergy and he founded the next parish near the new Cathedral of Mostar along the same lines. The people, who had been accustomed to the friars for centuries, refused to accept these changes even though such proceedure was quite normal in the Church).

Father Vego had stopped administering the sacraments, but he had not left Mostar as the Bishop had ordered. He visited Medjugorje from time to time where he prayed fervently. He returned just before Christmas 1981 and addressed Our Lady through Vicka requesting a message for his own guidance. Vicka repeated the Queen of Peace's advice to pray, because although Our Lady talked about reconciliation, more troubles and problems were arising. The Holy Mother added that the suspended friars were innocent and that such a decision had been hasty and that the Bishop should have solved the dispute more calmly. When the Bishop heard this he furiously denied that the Virgin Mary would ever criticize him and he changed his attitude towards the apparitions becoming a bitter enemy towards the happenings in Medjugorje.

As Vicka prepared for Christmas along with the other visionaries in Medjugorje, she was completely unaware that the answer she had relayed to Father Vego, in good faith, would have serious future consequences in her relations with the Bishop.

Our Lady, who was watching over Her chosen ones, gave them the following message three days before Christmas:

"Be on your guard, my children. Prepare yourselves for difficult days for all kinds of people will come here from all over."

Preparations for Christmas were more intensive that year than even before. Everybody was preparing to attend the Christmas Eve Mass. There was a blackout in the village that night and the stars lighted the way for those who were going to church. The altar was illuminated by two little bulbs, electricity supplied from the small well tank pump. The church was crammed full. Father Jozo Vasilj from Medjugorje celebrated the Mass. He was a man of great faith and culture who spoke many languages. During the Christmas Eve Mass he said:

"Jesus was born at the stroke of midnight and turned the night into day, He died by day and turned the day into the night. He resurrected at midnight and turned the night into the day but this is not the end of the story. Jesus still lives with us. There will always be Christians on the Earth, it only depends on you my brother my sister, if there will be one more or one less."

All the six visionaries took part in saying the rosary, they had the apparition and they retold the people about their everyday encounters with Our Lady which had now lasted six months. Christmas Eve Mass was unforgetable for the inhabitants of Medjugorje and the pilgrims who were present. They all sang their Christmas songs with all of their hearts and nobody felt like leaving the church to go home. Finally around two o'clock they started to go outside into the Christmas night walking in small groups towards their houses, softly singing "Silent Night, Holy Night" and other beautiful Christmas carols.

These parishioners, chosen by God, were living and experiencing extraordinary moments of grace.

On Christmas day, the Virgin Mary appeared in a shimmering golden dress to give them this message:

"Love one another, my children. You are brothers and sisters. Do not argue among yourselves."

Early January 1982, four of the visionaries left Medjugorje to return to school. That is when Our Lady started illustrating Her life in images to Vicka who diligently noted everything in an exercise book. This she will only publish when Our Lady gives Her the permission.

Father Slavko Barbarić

Having completed his studies in Pedagogy in Freiburg, Germany, Father Slavko Barbarić arrived in the parish of Medjugorje on 9th January, 1982. He exchanged greetings with his good friend Father Tomislav and immediately went to Bijakovići to meet the visionaries. In the late afternoon, when he returned to the parish office, he found a message from Father Tomislav which read as follows: "The police have taken me in, I do not know when I will be back. Prepare the Mass." Father Slavko made preparations, to the best of his ability, although he did not know anything about the programme before and after Mass. As for the apparitions, he was open-minded. He thought, if it happened in Fatima, why not in Medjugorje, too?

Two days after Father Slavko's arrival in the parish, Bishop Žanić appointed a committee to study the events of Medjugorje. That night, Our Lady told Vicka and Jakov:

"I invite you to participate in the Mass in a very special way. Wait for me in church, that is the best possible place!"

From that day onwards the two of them had the apparitions in the room opposite to the sacristy every evening. By the end of January they asked: "Our Lady why don't You leave a definite sign to convince the priests so that they will convert and then convert the others?" She replied:

"The sign will appear at the arranged time."

"Dear Lady, what should we do to stop the quarrels among the priests?"

"Fast and pray for this intention!" was the reply.

"Dear Lady when should we celebrate the Feast of The Queen of Peace?"

"I would prefer that it take place on June 25th. In fact the faithful came for the first time to the Podbrdo Hill that day."

By the end of February good news arrived. The Supreme Court of Bosnia and Hercegovina reduced Father Jozo Zovko's imprisonment sentence from three and a half years to two years. His lawyer was not satisfied with this partial success and appealed to the Federal Court in Belgrade.

Meanwhile Ivan had regular apparitions in the seminary. He too, was shown Paradise by our Lady and, while he was on this and other "trips" he could never be found by his companions ... he never talked about these experiences with anyone. He had problems studying but he tried hard. Unlike him, Mirjana was an excellent student even though she only lived for the moments of her meetings with Our Lady with whom she always prayed. The Virgin showed Her life to Mirjana and the other visionaries, just like She did to Vicka. As if in the movies, the scenes appeared in front of them. This helped them to consider Our Lady as their mother and friend.

For thirty days in a row Father Slavko talked with the visionaries immediately after the apparitions. None of them ever knew what they would be asked beforehand or who would be called first. However there were no inconsistencies, either with respect to the main messages or with respect to those received on that particular day. Father Slavko was intelligent, humorous, wise and profound and the childern soon became fond of him. Despite his out-going-personality, he never let his emotions take over when expressing his thoughts. This is why he managed to approach the group with the necessary professional distance. He was not prejudiced and had an open mind towards the happenings in Medjugorje.

The following is his first psychological analysis of the visionaries

"The visionary group was formed when Our Lady first appeared to them on June 25th 1981 and continued to exist even when the Parish Priest attempted to break them up. It is made up of youngsters who are fast growing up and their ages differ considerably. From their psychophysical constitutions we note that they are very different which is cause for amazement that they should form a group.

When I asked why they are together, they answered that Our Lady requires them to relay Her messages of peace to the world and call the world to conversion. They will do so as long as the Madonna requests it. Considering the fact that the course of events has virtually destroyed the private lives of these young persons and that they have to be in church for two or three hours every day and that time and again they have to retell the same things to the visitors, we can affirm that their personal interests have been ignored.

The stability of this group is an inexplicable phenomenon, therefore one should bear in mind what they say which is: that it is Our Lady who is keeping them together.

Description of the apparitions: suddenly, in the middle of the Lord's prayer, the visionaries kneel down as if struck by lightening. From that moment onwards, during the whole of the vision, they all stare at the same one point; they cease to communicate with the outer world. They claim, among other things, that they keep on speaking loudly although those who are present do not hear them. They are surprised about this because they claim they do not change the tone of their voice. Everyone who is there can see the visionaries moving their lips together if they ask something or individually if, as they affirm, they are speaking to Our Lady.

The essential content of the visions is prayer. Our Lady opens the prayer with "Lord's Prayer".... and they follow with "who art in Heaven", they skip "Hail Mary" which Our Lady never recites and immediately pass onto "Glory Be". After the prayers, they receive the messages and get the answers to their questions. They are often asked complicated questions that are beyond their intellectual capabilities, but to which they give answers that are coherent and meaningful."

Following the direct experience with the group of visionaries, Father Slavko concluded that all the six children were mentally sane persons, as a group and individually, so clearly healthy, normal children with normal human faults, Father Slavko, like the other authorities, bishops and relatives tried to find out more about Our Lady's secrets, but the children were silent. The only thing that Father Slavko managed to learn was that when a secret was intended for all of them, they all heard it, while when it was intended for one, only the chosen one heard it. One visionary told Father Slavko that she had been tempted to reveal one of the secrets once, but some inner voice prevented her from doing so.

Father Slavko, who was a pedagogue by profession, especially studied the apparitions through the prism of pshychology. He learned that Our Lady had suggested they all go into a convent or monastery because She considered that it would be the best solution for them. Slavko asked them if they had already chosen the place, to which they replied they were taking their time as they did not feel any obligation towards Her wish. The fact that the visionaries are able to distinguish between a specific request and simple advice from Our Lady confirms their mental health. Also their awareness of their free choice makes this group particularly special.

There is another interesting detail illustrating Our Lady's role as an educator: When the Holy Mother reproaches them She does so mildly, not changing Her expression or Her voice. If the fault concerns the entire group everybody hears it. If however it is intended for a single person, only he or she hears it. The others are aware of Her chiding, but not of what is said. Anyway a reproach always makes all of them feel rather embarassed afterwards. Father Slavko asked them if they knew they would be chided before the apparition and they answered that sometimes they had known and sometimes had not.

The Last Call to the World

After eleven months of apparitions, in early May 1982, Our Lady gave them an important message:
"I have come to call the world to conversion for the last time. Afterwards, I will not appear any more on this earth."

"Dear Lady, can we write down the date of the great sign in a sealed envelope and file it as the commission requires?"

"No! I have entrusted it only to you. You will reveal it when I tell you. Many will not believe you, I know, and you will suffer very much for it. But, you will endure everything and at the end you will be the happiest ones."

The first problems started when the Bishop questioned Vicka about the message referring to the suspended friars. He was not satisfied with her replies, he even accused her of lying, attributing to Our Lady words She had never said. Vicka replied that she would pray for him and he said that that was not necessary.

This was the period in which Vicka began to suffer from severe headaches, she would fall into a comatose state that lasted a long time. She would wake up for the apparition, and then afterwards remain unconscious for hours. Vicka was Jakov's major support, so now he felt alone and cried for her. During one of the apparitions Our Lady told him: "The cross is necessary to redeem the sins of the world."

Doctor Stopar, a famous psychiatrist, came to Medjugorje an the invitation from the friars. He visited the visionaries and gave a written report on them confirming that none showed any pathological symptom. He even hypnotized Marija. But, the girl's story was the same, whether she was conscious or hypnotized.

Several days before the anniversary of the apparitions, Father Tomislav wrote down Our Lady's messages in the Parish Chronicle, as Vicka relayed them:

"The most important thing is that you, the visionaries, remain united. Let peace be among you. Pay very close attention to this. Always be obedient and do what the priests and your parents tell you. Go to Holy Mass often and receive Communion. Be very attentive these days because many people will come to you in order to tempt you. Be careful of your statements. I'm expecting a very strict discipline from you these days. Do not go just anywhere, anytime, and do not separate from each other (one or two of the visionaries realised that these words were aimed at them particularly and they began to cry).

Our Lady continued: "A number of those who have been very enthusiastic will cool off. But you must persist and be proud of each one of my words. Have the people pray very much. Let them pray more for salvation, because salvation is in prayer. Let people be converted while there is still time. There are many sins, vexations, curses, swearing, lies and other evil false things. Let them be converted, go to confession and receive Holy Communion.

You have asked me to keep good and faithful priests in this parish who will continue the work. Do not be afraid of anything. This grace will be given to you. I do not demand anything other than prayers, perseverance and preaching from the priests that they may be patient and wait for the promises of God."

The answer to a theologian's question was noted, too:

"Has the Holy Spirit two natures?"

Through the visionaries the Virgin Mary replied:

"It has only one nature, Divine nature."

The visionaries asked again:

"Dear Virgin, You said that these apparitions were the last ones in the world?"

"Yes, these apparitions are the last in the world."

Everybody was very excited, both the visionaries and the parishioners, on the eve of the first anniversary of the apparitions. Everybody expected the great sign. They hoped for it and at the same time were afraid of it. Processions were arriving at Medjugorje all night long. Some of them had travelled for more than fifty kilometers but they were not tired. They only felt a kind of graciousness and happiness in their hearts because they arrived there and Our Mother the Queen of Peace was waiting for them. They had arrived "home". Marian songs were sung. The moon and stars shone brighter than ever. At dawn on 25th June the first "great" surprise occurred. The police let the people go to the Podbrdo Hill without any trouble. Again, it was unbearably hot, like the year before. The church was already full very early in the afternoon and people were flowing out into the churchyard. There were tens of thousands. All the visionaries were present. They were saying their rosaries when they experienced the apparition. Our Lady was full of bright light and dressed in gold. Here is the message of that day which was intended for the priests in particular:

"Thank the people in my name for the prayers, the sacrifices, and the penance. Have them persevere in prayer, fasting, conversion and have them wait with patience for the fulfilmet of my promise. Everything is unfolding according to God's plan."

The authorities were pleased to know that the Bishop was opposing the apparitions, they started to force the parishioners into paying "tourist tax" for the pilgrims they hosted in their homes. They would suddenly enter the houses and ask the pilgrims for their tax receipts. The pilgrims were usually poor people who had arrived on foot and of course there were no receipts because the parishioners did not charge the pilgrims at all! The parishioners had to pay heavy fines for "failure to pay tax". Some parishers were compelled to refuse hospitality to the pilgrims, others did not refuse the pilgrims: they paid the fines and still hosted them free of charge ... unafraid. Only a few families, who had larger houses and bathrooms, engaged in the tourism business. They charged low prices for lodgings which included tourist tax.

The authorities harassed the gypsies who put up their tents in front of the church and began selling pictures, rosaries, and statues. The inhabitants of Medjugorje were pleased about their being sent away because they considered that this trade was a major blasphemy. Very few of them had visited Rome or Lourdes and they did not know that in these internationally centers people made a living from such trading.

My grandmother Andja, who lived at Buna about 15 km from Medjugorje, heard of the apparitions. She believed in them and prayed very intensely for the intentions of Our Lady. One day her grandson Miljenko arrived from Banja Luka. He was passing by on business with two policemen.

Miljenko visited his (and my) grandmother and asked her if she needed something. She told him that she would like to go to Medjugorje, but she had no one to take her. Miljenko was embarrassed because he did not know how his police friends would react. He was about to say that they had no time but one of the policemen, an Orthodox, calmly said: "Let's take her there as she wishes so much to go there!" Grandmother Andja dressed quickly and said: "God, you are so great! It was only yesterday that the police harassed us for going to church, and today they want to take me straight to the Virgin!"

So they left and met a patrol at the entrance to Medjugorje. The police waved them to pass through and they were wondering what an old woman, dressed in black, was doing in a police car! They arrived at the church. Grandmother entered and thanked Our Lady ardently for this unexpected gift and then she prayed, first for her grandson and then for his friends who had made her wish come true. No one knows how they felt waiting outside the church.

My cousin was moved to tears, thinking about the inner strength which sustained our almost illiterate grandmother, who has always observed her faith and prayed not only for him, but also for all the family, her children and grandchildren. She always prayed to God to preserve us from all evil so that we will not lose our souls in the whirlpool of our worldly obligations which often leads to the denial of God's existence.

Interesting Replies

The Supreme Federal Court in Belgrade further reduced Father Jozo's sentence to a year and a half. In July the parishioners would have preferred to see Father Jozo already free. They continued to pray to God to give him strength sufficient to endure his imprisonment.

The Parish Chronicle mentions the apparitions in July and August 1982, when Our Lady responded to various questions regarding Purgatory:

"There are many souls in Purgatory. There are also persons who have been consecrated to God - priests and religious. Recite the Lord's Prayers, Hail Marys, and Glory Be at least seven times each, and the Creed. I recommend this to you. There is a large number of souls who have been in Purgatory for a long time because no one prays for them."

About fasting:

"The best fast is on bread and water. Through fasting and prayer one can stop wars and suspend the laws of nature. Charity cannot replace fasting. Those who are not able to fast can replace it with prayer, charity, and confession; but everyone, except the sick, must fast."

About the sick, for whom the visionaries prayed most frequently:

"For the healing of the sick, it is important to say the following prayers: the Creed, and seven times Our Father,

Hail Mary and Glory Be, and to fast on bread and water. It is good to impose one's hands on the sick and to pray. It is good to anoint the sick with Holy Oil. Not all priests have the gift of healing. In order to receive this gift, the priest must pray with perseverance and believe firmly."

About peace and reconciliation:

"One must invite people to go to Confession each month, especially the first Saturday. I have not spoken about it here. I have invited people to attend Confession. Frequently I will give you a few specific messages for your time. Be patient because the time has not yet come. Do what I have told you. Monthly Confession would be a remedy for the Church in the West. You must convey this message to western countries. "

On Assumption Day 1982, there were a great many pilgrims, who arrived from abroad too. The police stood at the village entrance noting car plate numbers. But, they did it with less attention and conviction than before. They penalised the local people whenever they could for accepting visitors in their homes. Many of the villagers seemed to be vaccinated, trusting in their luck not to be found out! It was so hot in the church that people could barely breathe. The friars installed an air fan but they had to disconnect it because the authorities said that it was "harmful for the people's health!"

Those who were outdoors felt a little better, although they had not enough room to kneel; very few could sit, but at least they had some air. In spite of all these difficulties, there was no anxiety, people smiled to one other, they felt relaxed. Regardless of discomfort and the heat, they felt as if they were reborn, like a sailor who returns home after sailing the world.

In the middle of all those people Our Lady approached the visionaries dressed in a golden dress.

The apparition lasted for seven minutes. Marija, Ivan, Mirjana and Jakov watched Our Lady speak to Vicka and Ivanka only.They realized that She was telling them a secret, but they did not hear what it was about.

Those who saw the visionaries that night noticed that Vicka and Ivanka were very serious. They tried to learn something from them, but in vain. The two girls had no intention of revealing the secret they had just received.

The following day, Our Lady told the visionaries that they and the people were praying too loudly and too fast, that they had to live the prayer intensely. Again, there were many questions about the sick. Our Lady repeated:

"I do not dispose of all graces! I received from God that which I have prayed for ... God has complete faith in me. I particularly protect those consecrated to me. The great sign has been granted. It will appear independently of the conversion of the people."

Some priests who had asked a question regarding the Pope, received the following reply:

"Have him consider himself the Father of all mankind and not only of Christians. Have him spread untiringly and with courage the message of peace and love among all mankind."

Sometimes Our Lady spoke a language unknown to them. Marija asked Her which language it was.

Blessed Virgin Mary replied:

"Aramaic, my mother tongue."

She prayed in Aramaic when there were people of Jewish origin in Medjugorje thus alluding to the role of this nation in Her plans.

Mirjana told about her experience one day while she was praying and waiting for Our Lady.

Satan suddenly appeared in front of her. He told her to renounce Our Lady, to follow him because he would make her happy in life and love. He also said that she would only suffer with Our Lady. Mirjana drove him away. Our Lady appeared immediately. The Blessed Virgin Mary asked the visionary to forgive Her for letting satan come, but She had had to show her that he really exists and that Mirjana had to live through this trial and it was necessary for her to see how horrible he was in all his wickedness.

Our Lady told Mirjana that satan had once gone to God's throne and had asked for permission to tempt the Church for a period of time.

God gave him permission to do so for an entire century (the twentieth).

When all the secrets, that Our Lady entrusted to the visionaries, have come true, his power will be destroyed.

Even now, satan has been losing and that is why he is so aggressive: he destroys marriages, stirs up quarrels among the priests, causes obsessions and murders, etc...

Defence lies in united prayer and holy objects, which we must carry around with us. It would be wise to return to the good old custom and sprinkle homes with Holy Water on Fridays.

The Gift of Interior Locution

Little Jelena, the second of the six children of the winegrower Grgo of Vasilj-Grgasović family and his wife Štefa, was nine when the apparitions started in Bijakovići. She believed in them immediately. In their patriarchal home near Križevac, the family frequently prayed and fasted led by grandmother and grandfather. Since the apparitions started they prayed even more frequently. Jelena was very attracted to prayer and to evening Holy Mass. One day she prayed from the bottom of her soul like this: "Oh, Lord, how happy I would be if I were able to believe only in You!"

After eighteen months of intensive prayers with her friends, Jelena heard an inner voice. It was Our Lady. Not only did she hear Our Lady's voice, but also she was able to see Her as well, although in a different way to the other visionaries. As after the initial wonder and surprise Jelena dared to ask the Queen of Peace if she too would be allowed to know the ten secrets. The answer came from an inner voice:

"I will not appear to you in the same way as I do to the other six because I have a different plan for you. I have entrusted messages and secrets to them. Forgive me for not being able to tell you the secrets too, but it is a grace intended for them alone. I will appear to you in order to help you develop in your spiritual life. I wish to lead other people to the light through you."

Father Tomislav questioned Jelena in order to understand how she heard Our Lady and how she felt when it happened:

"It is hard to describe. When I am with Our Lady it is as if I were on the phone; I can hear the others speaking in the room but I don't take any notice of them. I don't hear what they say because I'm completely concentrated on my "phone call!"

While one after another, the events in Medjugorje took their course the book "Apparitions of Our Lady in Medjugorje" was published by "Miriam" in Germany. The author was the priest Ljubić who had followed the apparitions from the very beginning. The book created great interest in all German speaking countries. The first edition sold out very quickly.

Mirjana continued to experience daily apparitions. She prayed with Our Lady and spoke with Her about the entrusted secrets. She beseeched Our Lady to save the world and this was the answer she received regarding the seventh secret:

"I have prayed and the punishment has been lightened. Continuous prayers and fasting mellow God's punishment, but it cannot be completely avoided. Go to the town and count those who praise God and those who insult Him. God will not accept it any more".

Two days before Christmas, Our Lady announced to Mirjana that She would appear to her for the last time. The visionary was very sad, she was afraid that she would not survive without the continual visions of Our Lady. The Blessed Virgin Mary came in splendour, in a golden dress and told her:

"From now on you will have to turn to God in faith like any other person. I will appear to you on the 18th of March every year and when you experience difficulties in life. Mirjana I have chosen you and I have confided in you everything that is essential. I have also shown you many terrible things. You must now bear it all with courage. Think of me and think of the tears I must shed because of this. You must always be courageous. You immediately accepted the messages. You must also understand now that I have to stop. Be strong!."

During that last daily apparition, which lasted for 45 minutes, Our Lady entrusted the tenth secret to Mirjana and told her when the secrets would come true. She told her that the terrible effects of the seventh secret had been considerably alleviated by the prayers and fasting that the people had offered.

Our Lady recommended her to choose a priest to whom she could reveal the secrets when the time came. Mirjana chose Father Petar Ljubičić (born 1946). Our Lady approved of the choice because She said Father Petar's heart was completely open to God. The other friars were surprised at this choice because Father Petar lived away from Medjugorje and hardly anybody noticed his presence when he visited. Thin, ascetic in appearance, he tirelessly gave confession to people outside the church. His eyes were clear and pious behind his glasses. His warm smile revealed his humble and modest person which enlightened all those who found themselves in his presence. The kind of person whom everyone would like to have as a brother. Here is Father Petar's comment:

"I was surprised that Mirjana chose me, for I am in service away from Medjugorje. But, she told me that, when the time comes, God will take care of everything. Our Lady has given Mirjana a kind of parchment paper on which are written the dates of the secrets. Ten days before revealing the first secret Mirjana will give me the parchment and I will be able to read the contents of the first secret, but only that one and not the others. Ten days later, just before revealing the secret, I must give back the parchment. Three days before the secret comes true, if I consider it necessary, I will reveal it to the world. The first two secrets will occur as a warning and also proof that Our Lady was really in Medjugorje. The third secret is a definite permanent sign which the visionaries have already seen. It is not known just how many secrets they know in common. This permanent sign will be announced three days before it appears. We should all prepare ourselves through prayer and fasting. Those who do this need fear nothing. "

The other visionaries received secrets as well as Mirjana. By early 1983 Marija had received seven secrets, Vicka eight, Jakov, Ivanka and Ivan nine. It is known that some of the secrets that Ivan received refer to his future. The children have revealed something about the third secret and only that one. They say it will be a visible sign on the Apparition Hill. It will be magnificent, tangible, real. After the sign has occurred Our Lady will only appear a few more times.

The news about this sign caused much excitement in Medjugorje and in nearby villages. They were expecting it any day and when this did not happen they cooled off, stopped fasting on Friday and attending Mass every evening. Hearts which had opened to the Holy Mother closed again. They had not understood Her messages about the importance of prayer because, had they prayed accordingly, they would certainly not have given such great importance as to when the sign would appear. Luckily there were many who were not interested in when exactly the sign would appear, in fact they were happy to have more time to strengthen their faith. Before returning to

Sarajevo, Mirjana visited Father Tomislav and told him of her fears ... of how she felt having been accustomed to the Madonna's presence for eighteen months ... of their intimacy ... and how She would no longer be appearing regularly as before.

Father Amorth,
famous exorcist, on
Apparition Hill

She, Mirjana, had been able to ask the Madonna any questions she wanted. One of these questions had been why God was so severe in condemning sinners to Hell. This was the answer:

"Those who go to Hell no longer want to receive any mercy from God. They do not repent nor do they cease to revolt and to blaspheme. They make up their minds to live in Hell and do not even contemplate leaving it."

So Mirjana understood that man punishes himself.

She also asked about Purgatory and receiving the following explanations:

"In Purgatory there are different levels; the lowest is closest to Hell and the highest gradually draws near to Heaven. It is not on All Souls Day but at Christmas that the greatest number of souls leave Purgatory. There are souls who pray ardently to God, but for whom no relative or friend prays on earth. God allows them to benefit from the prayers of other people. God may allow them to manifest themselves, in different ways, to their relatives on earth, in order to remind men of the existence of Purgatory and to solicit their prayers to God who is just and good. The majority of people go to Purgatory; many go to Hell; a small number go directly to Heaven."

After relaying the messages to the priest, Mirjana told him about herself and how her attitude towards religion has changed:

"While I was attending religious instruction, God was pictured as long bearded, very rigid, watching every mistake. I expected to be scolded for the slightest error. No priest ever depicted God as a good Father to whom I could confide all my problems. As a child, I was afraid of God, I thought he did not love me. Now I experience him as my Father who loves me so much and who lovingly corrects my mistakes when I do something wrong. Even when Our Lady invites us to become saints She does not ask much: She says that we should be convinced about what we are doing and should recite the rosary daily, help the weak, the poor and the old people joyfully rather than from a sence of obligation. I have prayed with Our Lady for non-believers and will keep doing so, because it is my mission."

After the apparitions stopped, Mirjana, who is a talentd artist, endeavoured to put Our Lady's image on paper using pencil and paints. But, every time she tried, she said that she was not able to express the immense beauty, fine features and love emanating from this heavenly creature. She also had to fight her depression because it was not easy to be in the company of Our Lady every day and then suddenly be without Her.

She endeavoured to live the messages she had received and feel the Heavenly Mother and Her Son Jesus in her heart.

After Mirjana returned to Sarajevo, she became more withdrawn and she sought solitude more and more. At school she was unable to follow classes and often she burst into tears. How could she explain that she cried because she no longer had the vision of the Holy Mother everyday as before? It was as if she suffered a great wound in her heart and she only found solace in her room, alone with her prayers to the Lady of Peace. In those moments she seemed to feel Our Lady praying with her.

Although the authorities did not give way and kept calling to account either the friars or the visionaries, the pilgrims kept arriving at Medjugorje. A TV crew arrived from the USA and they wanted to tape the apparitions. They had difficulty obtaining their permits, but in the end they succeeded in making a video. "Why do they want to take photos of us? We aren't film stars!" Ivanka protested, as she always did. As soon as Jakov saw a camera he would put his hands in front of his face. However, although the filming and photographs were embarrassing for them, the children realised that they were useful ways of spreading the messages throughout the world more rapidly.

The Frenchman canon René Laurentin, a great mariologist, who has written about eighty books on Mary's apparitions in the world, came to Medjugorje several times. During these visits, he talked with the friars and the visionaries. He spoke favorably of the events and he visited Bishop Žanić who vigorousgly opposed everything.

On returning to France, Laurentin wrote his book on Medjugorje and was surprised to hear that the first edition had been sold out very quickly. The surprise was even greater when he discovered that his book had inspired many men to convert. His readers wrote letters to him telling him how his book had inspired them to prayer and fasting and led them to God. René Laurentin was fully aware that all these conversions certainly did not depend on him, otherwise the same thing would have happened as a result of the other books he had written. Something special had happened.

The Persecution of Foreign Pilgrims

Father Jozo was released from prison in mid February 1983 and he went back to his parish for a short while. This is what he had to say about this experience :

"Every good priest should experience prison personally and suffer for his faith. There I met "the living dead" and I discovered how strong my Catholic faith was, which helped me to overcome continual, everyday difficulties. I realised how many irrelevant things I had considered important and how much time I had wasted on them. I tried hard to explain the word of God to the parishioners, but hardly anybody listened to me. Instead, when little Jakov said: "Let us recite the rosary" people accepted it with all their hearts. Only since then have I understood that Our Lady is among us. She converted me, too. Now I also understand those who say that they do not believe, because faith is a gift and, as such, must be obtained by prayer from God. A man without faith is like an airplane without the engine: he cannot fly. What does faith mean? It does not mean knowledge, it means obedience. The precondition for faith requires us to become as innocent as children. I invite you all to become the children of our Heavenly Mother and our Heavenly Father and obtain the gift of faith from Him through prayer. "

Inspired by Ljubić's book, five young students arrived from Austria that March. They were offered lodging in my cousin Miljenko's house and they made friends with his five children, as well as with Jelena and Marijana, their neighbours and parents. One of them was a medical student, Janez Mikl, a Slovenian by origin, and he managed to communicate with the natives in Slovenian.

On the sixth day of their stay, two of them went to Mostar and the other three went to Križevac with the Vasilj children.

On retourning from the hill, the police stopped them and asked them for their tax receipts for their board and lodgings. They admitted that they did not have any and, because they refused to say with whom they were staying, the police took them to Čitluk police station.

The police station was disorderly and noisy: the TV was on full blast; several telephones were ringing simultaneously and the room was full of cigarette smoke. Janez did not let the police know that he spoke Slovenian and that he understood what they were saying. The three young men were aware that the authorities were always suspicious and on the alert, eager to catch anyone organising a "counter-revolution".

In spite of the rather serious situation in which they found themselves all three of them felt no worry, instead they felt safe and protected. The police ordered them to leave Yugoslavia within the following twenty-four hours and they were forbidden to enter the country for at least three years. Jelena, Marijana and other children prayed for them all the time they were in Čitluk under questioning.

When young Janez got back to Vienna, he testified that he had experienced a rebirth of his old true faith at Medjugorje through reciting the rosary and through fasting. He was sad because he could not return to that blessed land and, inspired, he wrote the song: "Gospa, Majka moja, Kraljica Mira" (Madonna, My Mother, Queen of Peace...(this song is sung all over the world in Croatian in those prayer groups inspired by Medjugorje).

These were still precarious times. Therefore the authorities of the Franciscan Province decided that it was better for Father Jozo to be as far away as possible from Medjugorje. They sent him to a parish near Duvno and even there the police kept a strict watch on him.

Before Easter of that year 1983, Father Tomislav wrote a letter of protest to the police authorities because of all the hardships imposed on the parishioners. Before he could post it, Jelena, who knew nothing of his intentions, appeared saying:
"Don't protest against anyone or anything. When you have problems and difficulties, just smile and pray. When God commences His deeds no one can stop Him."

In the meantime, Jelena was getting used to her inner voice and she diligently informed Father Tomislav of the messages that she received which, without any doubt, were well beyond the understanding of this ten-year-old:

"Hurry and convert yourselves. Do not wait for the great sign. It could be too late then to convert. For those who have faith, this moment is a great opportunity to convert and strengthen your faith.

"Fast on bread and water before every Holy Day. Fast on bread and water once a week to the Glory of the Holy Spirit."

"My heart burns with love for you. All you have to do is convert. Hurry to proclaim it! Tell everyone that this is my request and that I will continually repeat it: convert ... convert! It is not difficult for me to suffer for you. I beg you, convert. I will pray to my Son to spare you the punishment. Convert without thinking twice about it. You do not know the plans of God. You cannot know them ... You cannot know what God will send or what He will do ... Therefore, I beseech you, convert. Renounce everything. This is part of the conversion. Peace be with you."

While praying together with Jelena, her cousin Marijana Vasilj saw Our Lady but did not hear Her voice. She was a pious girl who liked praying and she enjoyed reading the Holy Bible.

On 19th April 1983 the Holy Mother gave Jelena the following prayer which is now well-known:

"Oh Mother mine! Mother of goodness, love and mercy! I love You infinitely, and I offer myself to You. By means of Your goodness, Your love, and Your mercy, save me! I wich to be Yours. I love You infinitely and I beg You from the bottom of my heart to protect me.

Oh Mother of goodness, give me Your goodness, so that I can go to Heaven. I beg You through Your immense love to give me with Your grace so that I can love every person just as You loved Jesus Christ. I beg You fill me with the grace of being as merciful as You. I offer myself completely asking

You be with me every step I take, because You are full of grace. If I should lose Your grace, I beg You to help me find it again. Amen."

Rosy

A few days after Jelena received this spontaneous prayer, doctor Frigerio arrived from Milan accompanied by a colleague and Rosy, a midwife who had come to say thanks for her own miraculous recovery.

Six months previously Rosy had been on her death-bed because of cancer. The doctors in Milan could do nothing more for her, but doctor friends took her to Sweden to consult a famous specialist.

While they were waiting for the flight in the airport, Rosy was in agony and her sadness, her despair, warned them that she was well aware that the end was near. One of the doctors, Frigerio, couldn't stand to see her suffering so much. He said:

"This illness is not for death but for the glory of the Lord! There's a place in Yugoslavia where Our Lady has been appearing for over a year to six children. Now we'll go to Sweden and if something can be done, we'll go to Yugoslavia to thank Our Lady ... we'll go anyway because something will surely happen where the Madonna appears!"

In Sweden, a few minutes before the operation, Rosy told doctor Frigerio:

"If the operation fails, remember that I have written what I wanted to say to you on a piece of paper in my prayer-book." After this last sentence, she started losing consciousness because of the anesthesia. Doctor Frigerio, who was to assist the Swedish surgeon, wanted to take off his surgical gloves and mask and run away. He was very worried and the Swedish specialist was too, because the surgery was difficult and risky ... similar to another case where the patient had died after an extremely complicated operation lasting eighteen hours.

Rosy's operation took twelve hours: forty units of blood were used in transfusions and, when she finally opened her eyes, she managed to whisper: "I'm alive ... God is wonderful! ... It's a miracle!"

So, there they were in Medjugorje to keep their promise. Before leaving Milan they had spoken to the editor of the Catholic weekly magazine "Il Sabato". The editor Farina had asked his friend Frigerio to take some photos of the visionaries. So doctor Frigerio introduced himself to Father Tomislav as a collaborator for the Italian publication, who had come to thank Our Lady for Rosy's recovery and participate in the apparitions.

He also asked the friar to deliver a request from some doctors working in the largest maternity hospital in Milan who, through 'Il movimento per la vita' (the pro-life movement) were opposing the legalization of abortion.

Little Jakov, after the apparition that evening, went to sister Janja, a nun, pointed to doctor Frigerio and started to speak to her in Croatian. The nun approached the doctor and asked in English if he were a gyneacologist, on his confirmation the nun communicated the following message:

"Our Lady blesses you and all those who work with you in the Milanese hospital for the good that you are doing. You must continue with your endeavours, you must pray. Our Lady blesses the sick in your hospital, those for whom you have prayed this evening and those for whom you will pray in the future."

The next day, on the way home, doctor Frigerio stopped in Split and visited Archbishop Franić, who told him:

"Since the happenings of these last two years in Medjugorje more has been achieved than by us bishops of Yugoslavia in twenty years! It would be helpful if you, doctor, could assist us by studying and analysing the cases of miraculous recoveries of which we have medical records."

Doctor Frigerio took the Archbishop's request very seriously and as soon as he returned to Milan, he contacted doctor Mario Botta, an expert and member of the medical committee for miraculous recoveries in Lourdes.

He informed his friend Farina of his visit to Medjugorje and the editor set off for Medjugorje himself to witness the significance of Our Lady's apparitions. Here is what Farina later said about his experience in Medjugorje:

"I approached the visionary Marija and told her with the help of Father Vlašić that we had heard she and the other visionaries would only reveal the secrets to the Church Authorities. Marija looked me straight in the eyes and calmly replied that she would reveal the secrets only when and to whom Our Lady ordered. At that precise moment I was certain that the children were telling the truth. I have not written it in "Il Sabato" but here I will say it! I was touched to tears ... perhaps Our Lady really would appear that evening, so near to me! I am obliged to say "perhaps" probably because of my profession but I have cancelled the word "perhaps" in my heart."

Thanks to this, many Italians began to be interested in the apparitions and from that moment hundreds of pilgrims began coming to Medjugorje non-stop. There were even more people present on the second anniversary. They prayed and sang all night long. The church was open and people slept on the church pews, in the churchyard and in the square. The pilgrims from abroad stayed in all the hotels in Čitluk, Ljubuški, Mostar, Čapljina. The authorities ordered the Franciscans to discourage the people from going to the Podbrdo Hill. Then, suddenly, the situation changed completely: orders arrived allowing people to climb the hill. Witnesses say that there were more than one thousand people going up the Apparition Hill.

Two books were published that summer; one in Croatian: 'The apparitions of Our Lady in Medjugorje', by the theologian Ljudevit Rupčić. The other in English, by Father Svetozar Kraljević, which was published in Canada. The latter was immediately translated into French.

The book in Croatian caused great trouble to the author, Father Rupčić, who was threatened with inprisonment. He was not in the least bit afraid for he had already experienced the hardships of communist prisons. Luckily he was not imprisoned but they took his passport away for six years.

The divine events continued to bear their fruits as the visiting foreigners coming to Medjugorje were able to witness. Here is a story told by doctor Marzia Monaj from Milan:

"On the night between 9th and 10th August 1983, I was travelling by train from Milan to Palermo. At about 11 p.m., I lay down in my couchette, said a prayer to Our Lady and thanked Her for everything I had experienced during my pilgrimage to Medjugorje from 31st July to 5th August. I fell asleep immediately. I don't know what time was, but just before arriving in Bologna, I had a clear dream: two trains seemed to be going to run into each other and in the distance, a bright shining female figure appeared. She was wearing a grey-blue gown and a white veil. Her arms were just slightly open. I could not see Her face; then, with a slow calm questure She made a sign to the train as if asking it to slow down.

Everything suddenly seemed much nearer. I could see the gown quite clearly but the Lady's face was so bright that I could not distinguish anything, except for a serious expression on a face that was sweet and serene. The figure blessed the train. At this point I saw the train driver pulling desperately at the brakes and then cover his face with his hands. When I woke up the train had stopped at Bologna.

The next day I was surprised to read that a bomb had been placed on the Milan-Palermo line and had exploded in front of the 571 Express... instead of underneath ... thus avoiding by a miracle a mayor accident. At first I did not realise the connection between my dream and what had happened.

It was only while reading the newspapers that I discovered the incredible coincidences of certain details in my dream and the "very near" tragedy. I managed to track down the train driver, Maletti, who looked exactly like the train driver in my dream! He was almost shocked when I described to him exactly how he pulled the brake and then covered his face with his hands. He confirmed this behaviour explaining that splinters of glass from the window had hit his face. When I asked what had made him brake so suddenly, he said "I saw a notice telling me to slow down immediately!"

The news of Our Lady's apparitions often appeared in the Italian press but I had little time for reading newspapers. I was on our family holiday in Croatia with my children and mother-in-law who was slowly recovering from a stroke.

When we arrived at Opatija my parents gave me Father Rupčić's book. I read it at once and it reminded me of the children of Fatima: Lucia, Jacinta and Francisco.

I had often read about them when I was a child and I imagined their happiness while they were meeting Our Lady.

Here it was! Happening again! A few lucky children were seeing Her, and would you believe it? At Medjugorje! At my ancestors village!

How I wished that I too could go there! I devoted myself to my sick mother-in-law who, thanks to the healthy sea air, gradually got better with every day that passed.

When my husband eventually joined us I confided my deep desire to visit Medjugorje and to my joy, he decided we should all go: he, my mother-in-law, our two children and I.

We arrived in Medjugorje just after Assumption Day. I expected to see many people, but I was surprised to see the church square humming with Italian, German, and Croatian pilgrims dressed in jeans and national costumes. With difficulty we managed to make our way through the long line of people going towards Križevac to the Vasilj's house where my father was born.

My uncle Janko had put water, wine and figs on a stool in front of his house as an offering to those who were passing by. I had never seen him so happy before.

Many years had passed and here I was again, in my father's house, meeting young cousins who had been born during my nineteen years' absence. I was pleasantly surprised to see how respectful the young people were towards the elderly ... something you rarely see now in the western socalled "civilized" countries! The houses were open day and night. Nobody locked their doors. Everyone lived as patriarcal families: grandparents, sons, wives and numerous children.

During Summer evenings the young people would meet up together at a place called "the stacija" on the road leading to Križevac. Here they would laugh and joke together and talk about the day's happenings.

My young cousin Silvana told me about an experience she had shared with some other people just a few days before I arrived. She said:

"The other evening at about 10 o'clock I felt an irresistable urge to go outside. I sat down on the terrace and casually gazed towards Podbrdo Hill, just as a bright light seemed to engulf the hill itself. Then it bathed the whole village until it slowly faded away. Suddenly there was a strange, loud noise like the sound of a storm ... then ... silence again. The bright light reappeared seeming to expand everywhere and there, in the very centre, was a cross from which rays of light shone, illuminating surroundings.The cross transformed into the form of Our Lady. I was moved to tears as I whispered: thank You for this wonderful gift!"

That very same evening that we arrived at Medjugorje all five of us: husband, mother-in-law and children, went to church which was crammed full of pilgrims and we had, with difficulty, to find a place standing up in the square outside.

The rosary was already being recited as I asked myself when I had last recited it. I remembered now, as a child refugee, I had always participated in the evening vespers ... everyday ... until I was about fourteen. At High School I only remembered my faith on Sundays when I went to Mass. At this moment I realized the emptiness around me and inside of me. How long would it last if I continued to seek life's values where they were not to be found?

How many years of intolerance towards myself and others had elapsed? How could I ever even begin to understand the meaning of life without delving into my very soul? There, before the church of Medjugorje, I was taken back, once more, onto the path that leads to God ... a path which I already knew ... but a path that I was following with distraction and uncertainty ... never realising that I was losing myself.

Here I was ... a woman of forty ... who suddenly discovered the child within ... that same child who had prayed so deeply and sincerely, at the age of ten, kneeling in front of a drawing of the Holy Mother and Her child in an old cellar.

Was it, perhaps, that beautiful pure prayer that had saved me from all the serious problems and dangers I had encountered in my life up till that moment? Was it that very prayer which was helping me to understand how humble one should learn to be, so as not to stray from one's faith?

The next day, I climbed the Apparition Hill barefooted, yet I did not scratch myself on a single thorn bush. My husband and children were with me while my mother-in-law was looked after by my grandaunt Anica.

My mother-in-law was happy, you could see it by her smile and it was clear that she too felt something in her soul.

On that second night of our stay I managed to enter the church with my daughter Lara. The heat almost suffocated us, people were pressing from all sides, and almost lifting us from the ground. A little old woman, dressed in rough black wool moved in front of us. She smelt strongly of body odour and, as I tried to pull back from her, she turned to me, looking me straight in the eyes and gently said:

"My child, it wasn't my intention in coming all this way to disturb or bother you!"

She was mild, humble and kind. I felt a lump in my throat as the tears flowed freely from my eyes. Something melted within me ... I learned an important lesson ... Since then such things have never ever bothered me again.

The following morning, I discovered that there was a Mass in Italian in the room next to the altar in church. During the sermon, Father Tomislav reported briefly on the events of those last two years. I was happy for my husband and mother-in-law because the Mass was in their language.

It never occured to me to ask myself where all the Italians were coming from nor did I have any wish to get to know them.

Instead, I was interested in the evening pilgrim Mass in Croatian. That evening a well-known spiritual healer, Father Emiliano Tardif from Domenican Republic, would be present. He prayed for the sick and I witnessed the instant healing of many with my own eyes during his prayer. We all sang Glory, Glory, Hallelujah! together.

My daughter Lara, who was suffering from serious circulation problems, asked me if there was any chance that she might recover. I replied that she certainly might if it were God's will. Very early next morning, I was in church with my mother-in-law and my daughter.

We were alone sitting in the first pew in front of the altar. Father Tomislav and Father Tardif arrived and went to the chapel of the apparitions. About ten minutes later both priests came out of the chapel and I saw that tears were streaming down the face of Father Tardif.

As yet I was unaware that the police had ordered him to leave Yugoslavia within twenty-four hours.

A special and memorable experience for me was the prayer with my ten year old cousins Jelena and Marijana. They would kneel on the floor for hours, saying the rosary with deep devotion and mediteting on the mysteries.

They would read passages from the Gospels and discuss them. Where did such wisdom come from? I realised that it came from their inner voice ... that Our Lady granted them their peace and prepared them for their prayers.

I asked Jelena several questions:
"What is meditation for you?"
"Our Lady has led me frequently. She has advised me to read any chapters from the Gospels and to compare them with my life to reflect and ask Jesus what I am doing wrong. In that way, I understand clearly where I'm going wrong and how I can correct myself. Then from the depth of my heart, I thank Jesus for His help. This is what I call meditation."

"When did you establish the prayer group?"
"At the end of May Our Lady told me to inform the priest that it was necessary to establish a prayer group in the village. There are fifteen of us now, we meet on Tuesdays. The Queen of Peace recommends three hours of prayer, and fasting too."

"Could you have ever imagined you would have been able to pray so much as you do now, before the apparitions occurred?"

"Since Our Lady has been with us, many things are much clearer. Other people in the parish also had the same opportunity as us to find peace in their souls through prayer.

Some say that they have found it, but this is not always true.

Our Lady says that although they have had this opportunity many have missed it! ... At first they were enthusiastic but then they did not persevere.

Many have thought: 'The Holy Mother is here, She will take care of everything'. Although many claim that they attend Mass gladly, in their hearts they do not accept Her messages completely and do as She wishes."

"Does the Virgin Mary leave you to pray as you please?"

"At the beginning She said: "Pray if you want to". Now She says: "Pray because, if you do not pray now, you will be sorry later. You can not understand what it will mean if you leave this path now."

"Does the Virgin Mary teach you the spiritual life?"

"Yes. In the beginning I used to write down what She said and that confused me. Then Our Lady told me to stop writing, that She would lead me through interior locution and that there would be no difficulty in following Her advice. When we sin we become afraid and it is this fear which leads us away from Her and Jesus."

This is why it is necessary to pray ... because prayer purifies the heart. If we pray, Jesus 'returns' in our hearts because we cannot expect Him to be born again in a manger.

"Is there something you feel you should add to this?"''

'The thing that most surprises me and that gives me the greatest joy is the fact that I now consider the Holy Virgin as my mother, Jesus as my friend ... my brother and God as my Father! I realize that God does not wish me to neglect my friends but rather to show them, through my prayers, just how important God is in my life."

Up till that moment I had never heard such wise replies from anyone of her age and it was another sign to me that I should believe in the apparitions of Our Lady.

On the last day of our stay, I went to Mostar with my children and bought some silver crosses for the seven god-children that I have scattered all over Europe. I put them in an envelope with their names written on it and left the envelope in the chapel just before the visionaries entered. Then I returned to the church. When I went to pick up the envelope after Mass, I could not find it. I was very sorry because I had no time to buy more crosses and have them blessed again. I was also sad because I was leaving Medjugorje to go back to Italy and I had no idea when it would be possible to return. However I thanked God for the gift of that visit.

On arrival home, I realised that visiting Medjugorje was a relatively easy matter ... what was difficult was actually putting the Madonna's teachings into practice in my daily life.

I thought about the illnesses of my daughter and mother-in-law, my duties as a housewife and mother, everything seemed an obstacle against finding those precious moments to pray ... regularly. I was afraid that the same thing would happen to me as the Holy Mother had forecast in Her messages:

196

"Some start by praying and fasting but they tire of this and lose the grace they have achieved."

The only connection I had with Medjugorje were the letters I received from my young cousin Silvana that was how I learned that Jakov's mother had died and that Our Lady had comforted him by saying that she was in Paradise with Her. Silvana also wrote saying that her distant cousin Marijana, like Jelena, had began to receive Our Lady's messages through interior locution. Our Lady presented herself to Marijana as the Mother of Goodness, Love and Charity and gave her the following message:

"See how happy I am here where there are many who honor me. Do not forget however that there are still many who offend and sadden me... Be careful and do not limit yourself to prayers alone ... satan is enraged against those who fast and convert to God. I want peace and love to grow in you. Pray! I love you but how much of my love you receive depends on you!"

I was delighted for Marijana and for the wonderful gift she had received. In my opinion this proves my point regarding the authenticity of the visions of the six children. Jelena and Marijana first accepted Our Lady's messages and with all their hearts they had prayed and fasted and only then did they receive the gift of interior locution. This indicates that sincere, heartfelt prayer can bring great spiritual fruits.

I also learned, from another of Silvana's letters that Our Lady had suggested, through Jelena, that the prayer group should set a period of four years, in which to pray intensely and reflect carefully, so that each one of them could then make the right decision for their future. The blessed Mother Mary advised them to pray to the Holy Spirit so that it might descend on them ... for with such grace all things are possible. At first the group consisted of Jelena and Marijana's friends and cousins. Gradually, other members were enrolled. One of the friars would often pray with them when free of other duties. It was on 28th November 1983 that Jelena received two prayers of consecration through her inner locution:

"O Immaculate Heart of Mary, overflowing with goodness, show us Your love for us. May the flame of Your heart, Oh Mary, descend upon all peoples. We love You immensely. Impress true love in our hearts so that our hearts may yearn for You always. Oh Mary, sweet and humble of heart, remember us when we sin. Through Your most sacred and pure heart, give us spiritual health. Make us for ever able to recognize the beauty of Your maternal heart: and, in doing so, be converted to the flame of Your heart. Amen."

Marijana Vasilj

"O, Jesus, we know that You are forgiving, that You have offered Your Heart to us. It is crowned with thorns and our sins. We know that You still pray for us so that may not be lost. Through Your most Sacred Heart, help us all to love one another and let all hatred disappear from mankind. Show us Your love. All of us love You, we desire that You protect us with Your Heart of Good Shepherd and free us from all sin. Enter into each heart, Jesus! Knock ... knock on the door of our hearts. Be patient and tenacious with us. Our hearts are still tighly closed because we do not understand Your love. Knock continuously. Oh Jesus. Make our hearts open up to You, at least when we remember what You suffered on the cross for us. Amen."

Pilgrims from Lecco

Six months after my return to Italy, while I was in a doctor's waiting-room with my mother-in-law, I started up a conversation with a lady sitting next to me. When she learned that I was a Croatian, she asked me if it were true that Our Lady was appearing in my country. I replied that in my opinion it was true: she took a piece of paper from her purse and showed it to me. It was a printed article containing information that Father Tomislav had given to an Italian group. They had probably taped his voice then written down his words and photocopied it. There was a phone number on the paper which I copied down.

When I arrived home I thought about calling to the phone number which was in Lecco, a town nearby. I wanted to know if anyone were going to Medjugorje so that I could ask if they would get me some more silver crosses for my godchildren and have them blessed. Somehow I felt responsible for these children; I was their godmother; to me it was important.

So I telephoned to Pietro Voltan in Lecco and when I told him that I was from Medjugorje he was so excited that he started to stutter. He said that he wanted to meet me, along with his friend Alberto Bonifacio, who was also very interested in the apparitions.

This is how I met the pilgrim group from Lecco. They had made a video about the visionaries and the Holy Mother during their recent visit to Medjugorje. The film contained much material in Croatian. They also had religious printed material in Croatian, and it seemed as if were there waiting to be translated by me. Immediately, I set to work translating everything for them. I also translated messages and prayers that Jelena had received through interior locution. I translated the hymn of Medjugorje as well.

The group, led by Alberto Bonifacio, went from parish to parish giving witness to the happenings in Medjugorje. They also showed their video and I was very touched to relive my own experiences through seeing it.

It showed the visionaries during the apparitions in the chapel, where I myself was not allowed to enter. I thanked the Holy Mother for this opportunity to share with them and was no longer sorry that I had not witnessed it personally in Medjugorje.

Meeting people from Lecco was a pleasant discovery for me. I have never believed in coincidence as I have aslways sought the links and relationships between things and happenings.

When in Medjugorje, I had listened to the friars speaking in Italian, German, English and in Croatian but I had never heard them tell the pilgrims to organize themselves in groups and to communicate the Holy Mother's messages. Yet, spontaneously, out of gratitude, the Lecco group were doing this!

That was when I realised that the Gospel is, itself, the "Good News"! Without need of direct organised publicity because it announces itself!

It was clear to me that I was being given a second chance to convert along with the extraordinary possibility to witness the presence of Our Lady amongst us!

I listened carefully to the testimonies of the people in the Lecco group ... of their renewed faith in God.

Alberto Bonifacio spoke of how in tune he felt with the Holy Mother's messages. Messages that he felt were vibrant, modern, personal and above all convincing.

He started writing articles for the Catholic Press, he established a prayer group and was amazed at how many people joined it! Many converted while they were listening to the testimonies, they started fasting and praying regularly in their families.

Not only Alberto, but most of the pilgrims who visited Medjugorje, found that people literally hung onto their every word about Medjugorje. A man called Carlo was there too. Here is his testimony:

"In Medjugorje the Church prays as the Queen of Peace requests. I saw young people on their knees and I kneeled with them and I asked the Lord to forgive me for all the times I've failed to do so in the past. Our Lady tells us that if we want peace we must kneel and ask the Lord for it!"

While listening to these testimonies, it was clear to me that the greatest help that we can give each other is to open our hearts without fear and let them speak the language of love. So I took my courage in my hands and I began talking about my experience of faith, that faith which I now knew was steady and strong not because I came from Medjugorje but because it was due to Our Lady's help, Her work on me ... for She wishes us to help Her, through prayer and testimony, to conduct mankind to God.

Every time I had to speak in public, I had butterflies in my stomach but I did it just the same, feeling it was my duty, as I lived so near Lecco where so many Italian pilgrims left for my ancestorplace: Our Lady's sanctuary.

I met a couple from Lecco who went to Medjugorje out of pure curiosity. On arriving at the church, they asked themselves why they were there. The answer came to them. They were there to ask Our Lady to help them adopt a child. It was their great wish, even though they already had three children of their own.

As soon as they returned to Lecco they read about an offer to adopt two children who were both sick. They felt they could not refuse and they offered to have both children. It was not a decision made because they were wealthy, quite the opposite. It was made because they believed in God and His generous providence. Their good will was required which they reenforced at Medjugorje. Otherwise they could have found so many excuses as to why they should not go in for that particular adoption.

As for me, I was blessed with an unexpected miracle. In spite of my numerous obligations, I found help in my home, so in spring 1984 I could return as a volunteer-guide for pilgrims. Leaving for Medjugorje I relived the experience of my first visit and I was given the oppotunity to meet the visionaries personally. Vicka was very sick, so Marija, who had finished school, took her place. Although she was timid, she gladly responded to people's questions. Her gentle voice revealed her will to relay Our Lady's messages as faithfully as possible.

Marija thin and skinny, radiated a kind of inner beauty and I was fascinated when she described how once, during prayer, she had seen a flower with its head bent down, petals closed ... as if it were dying. Marija then saw a drop of water fall onto the withered flower. Its life returned and the flower opened up in all its beauty, fulli blossomed and full of light. Marija asked Our Lady what the vision meant. She replied that the flower represented the soul which flourishes with the grace of God, but dries and withers when we fall into sin.

While my Italian group and I were with Marija, a group of Germans arrived. They did not have an interpreter so Marija patiently waited while I translated everything she said into the two languages. We learned from her that a group of young people had visited Pope John Paul II and that they had given him a wooden cross on which was inscribed the messages of Our Lady: peace - prayer - fasting - conversion.

She also confided that for some time she had started to receive messages for the parish every Thursday. The first such message was received on March 1, 1984. We asked her to tell us the message. Here it is:

"Dear children! I have chosen this parish particularly because I wish to lead it. I am guarding it with love and I want everyone to be mine. Thank you for your response this evening. I would like you to be with my Son and me in ever greater numbers. I shall give a special message to you every Thursday."

Invitation to Enter the Prayer Group

During the summer of that same year, 1984, I managed to stay in Medjugorje with my daughter Lara for several weeks. The yards in front of Jelena and Marijana's houses were full of foreign pilgrims every day.

Marijana's six-year-old sister Anita asked me what languages these people spoke and I replied: German, Italian, English, French. She thought for a moment and said:

"All these different languages yet they all keep asking the same question: "What does the Holy Mother say?" How come they don't understand once and for all that She only says pray, pray, pray!"

I discussed the changes in the village with my relations. Whether they wanted them or not, the inhabitants of Medjugorje were obliged to become the hosts of bed and breakfast establishments. They could no longer offer lodgings free of charge because the authorities kept insisting they pay a "tourist tax".

However, they asked for very little or the pilgrims themselves made a donation. The very first pilgrims had no particular needs and their only desire was to be able to pray together with their host family. Many, especially the young, helped the peasants working in the fields. One young doctor insisted on milking a cow!

Marijana's father, who worked in Germany had an excellent idea to help develop the village. He thought it would be a good idea to build a new house, built of stone to host the pilgrims. He felt it could be built at the foot of the Križevac Hill towards Mount Crnica. A few foreigners also tried to go about building large guest-houses with the help of the local people. They would be used by the visiting pilgrims.

One of the first to succeed was Marina Cagnoni from Milan. She had a large house built on the Križevac-Miletina road and it accommodates approximately fifty pilgrims.

The land near the parish house was government property which had been confiscated from the friars by the authorities, immediately after the war. The friars attempted, in vain, to buy the land back from the local community officers. They refused to sell. Instead they leased it to people who came from Zenica, Sarajevo, Šabac and Požarevac allowing them to put up their tents, live there with their families and sell souvenirs.

The community allowed the construction of several large buildings near the church and it was clear that they intended to seek financial gain from a religious situation they seemed unable to subdue.

Those inhabitants of Medjugorje who owned land near the church were quick to realise that, if they did not act quickly, the authorities might very well confiscate their lands too, turning them into "public" property. So together they quickly built guest-houses around the church.

In the third year of the apparitions there were more and more Yugoslav tourist guides in Medjugorje. This fact alone confirmed how the attitude of the authorities was changing. These guides spoke foreign languages, but knew very little about religion, and only God Himself knows how they managed to translate what they heard from the visionaries. One thing is certain: God had His plan; in fact some of these guides converted.

I often visited the visionary Marija during that summer. She told me that she had started working as a hair stylist in Čitluk and had liked the job. But, the zealous Italians had found her even there and had made it impossible for her to keep her job. However their pestering had a good side to it because she began learning Italian. I felt sorry for her; because she did not have a moment to herself.

Her house was literally "besieged" by pilgrims who were obviously unaware how selfishly they were behaving, forgetting that they were not the only ones who were stealing her precious time.

One afternoon, I found myself at Jelena's place, she, as usual, was in her room with her cousins, praying fervently. While I was talking with her parents, a girl from the group came out of the room where they were praying and asked me to enter. Jelena was expecting me and smiled as I sat down at her invitation. She had a message for me. Our Lady told her: "Mirjana loves me very much even though she sometimes forgets all about this love for me!" I was very touched by what She said and, while my eyes filled with tears I whispered: "Thank you dearest Mother for You are always there waiting patiently for me." When the prayers ended, Marijana said that we should find a quiet place, contemplate on the messages we had received and prepare for Holy Mass.

I went to the back room of the old family house and sat in silence by the window. Under a log, by the garden fence, a small snout peeped out. I felt a gush of spontaneous love for the little animal even though it turned out to be a rat. I felt no revulsion ... was this because my heart had been opened to everything created by God?

Father Petar Ljubičić joined us in prayer the following day. So I had a chance to meet him and understand why the visionary Mirjana chose him of all the priests. He was completely devoted to living Our Lady's messages and he radiated peace, goodness and love. He was as happy as a little child when Jelena told him that Our Lady had blessed us all and that She had put invisible golden rosaries around our necks as a sign that we belonged to Her and She wished us to pray for Her intentions.

During the prayer, Marijana and Jelena taught us all how to meditate on the "Lord's prayer" according to the heavenly Mother's guidance:

Our Father! - Who is this Father? Of whom is he the Father? Where is this Father? This is our Father. Why are you afraid of Him? Hold out your hands to Him. Our Father means that He has given Himself to you as a Father. He has given you everything. As your earthly Father does for you so much more will your heavenly Father do.

Who are in Heaven! This means that your earthly Father loves you but your heavenly Father loves you more. Your earthly Father can get angry: but your heavenly Father does not; He offers you only His love .

Hallowed be Thy Name! In return you must respect Him, because He has given you everything and because He is your Father and you must love Him. You must glorify and praise His name. You must say to sinners: He is the Father;

yes, He is my Father and I wish to serve Him and to glorify only His name. This is the meaning of "Hallowed Be Thy Name".

Thy Kingdom come! This is how we thank Jesus and say: Jesus, we know nothing; without your Kingdom, we are weak if our kingdom ends, while Yours is eternal. Establish it once more!

Thy Will be done! O Lord, make our kingdom collapse. Let Your Kingdom be the only true one, and make us realise that our kingdom is destined to end and that at once, now, we allow Thy Will to be done.

On earth as it is in Heaven! Lord, as the angels obey you, make us obedient like them ... open our hearts so that we respect You in the same way as the angels do ... and make everything as holy on earth as it is in Heaven.

Give us this day our daily bread! - Give us, Lord, food for our souls; give it to us today, give it to us always; that this food be sanctified by You, may this food become eternal. O Lord, we beg You to give us your bread. O Lord, make us worthy to receive of it. O Lord, help us to understand what we should do once we have eaten of Your bread. Help us to realize that our daily bread cannot be received without prayer.

And forgive us our trespasses! - Forgive us our sins Lord. Forgive us if we are not always as good and faithful as we should be.

As we forgive those who trespass against us! Forgive us so that we, too, may forgive those that we have not been able to forgiving until now. O Jesus, forgive us our sins we beseech You. Referring to us, pray that your sins may be forgiven you in the same measure as you forgive those who trespass against you. This is what your Heavenly Father is telling you with these words: forgive if you wish to be forgiven.

Lead us not into temptation! - Lord, free us from difficult trials. Lord. we are weak. Do not let our trials, O Lord, lead us to ruin.

But deliver us from evil! - Lord, free us from evil. Help us to find the hidden blessings present in our trials so that we can develop in our lives.

Amen! - So be it, Lord, Thy Will be done!

On 23rd September, 1984 Our Lady taught Jelena and Marijana how to recite the rosary of Jesus which the group have repeated together on bended knee, since that day. First the Creed is recited and then the seven mysteries. After every mystery, the Lord's Prayer is repeated five times and the invocation: "O Jesus, be our protection and strength!"

> 1st mystery: Let us contemplate the birth of Jesus.
> Intention: let us pray for peace.

> 2nd mystery: Let us contemplate Jesus' help to the poor.
> Intention: Pray for the Pope and the bishops.

> 3rd mystery: Let us contemplate Jesus' trust in God's Will.
> Intention: Let us pray for priests and all those who serve Jesus in a special way.

> 4th mystery: Let us contemplate Jesus' sacrifice for us through His love.
> Intention: Let us pray for the family.

> 5th mystery: Let us contemplate how Jesus gave his life for us.

Intention: Prayer that we are able to open our hearts to everyone.

6th mystery: Let us contemplate Jesus' victory over satan and evil. Intention: Let us pray that our hearts become free of sin and all chains so that Jesus may be resurrected in our hearts.

7th mystery: Let us contemplate Jesus' Ascension. Intention: Let us pray that God's Will is done.

Before reciting seven "Glory Be" contemplate how Jesus sent the Holy Spirit.

Intention: Let us pray for the gift of the Holy Spirit.

Miljenko Vasilj's family with pilgrims

The Apparitions in the Church
Are Prohibited

The Italian pilgrims were sorry to hear that Father Tomislav had left for Vitina, a village that is fifteen kilometres from Medjugorje. They followed him there and this created problems with the authorities both ecclesiastical and civil for the good friar.

His position in Medjugorje was taken over by Friar Slavko Barbarić whom the visionaries knew and liked well. He spoke several languages and was untiring. He wrote numerous books regarding the Holy Mother's messages the first of which bears the title "Pray with the heart". He often substituted for the old organist when the heat in summer was unbearable. He sang well and also played the guitar in the company of young people.

Barbarić soon became the focal person for the various groups of pilgrims, the visionaries and local inhabitants. You could say that he became 'the Parish Priest' for all the pilgrims from all over the world. Because of this, because of his great culture and charisma he earned the enmity of Medjugorje's enemies. The police could not bring any accusations against him. Being of natural open attitude with a fine sens of humor, he was always courteous and pleasant to the government officials thus never jeopardizing his position.

Yet, he experienced growing difficulties with the Church Authorities, especially with the Bishop who stated that he would go on his knees from Mostar to Medjugorje if the apparitions of Our Lady were proved true. On hearing this Father Slavko commented: "Poor Bishop, perhaps he does not know just how long that journey is, it will not be easy for him!"

The Bishop banned the apparitions in the church and he forbade his priests to talk about the messages from the altar. So the daily meetings of the visionaries took place in the parish house. The pilgrims' letters were archived in that room so it soon became a kind of communication center with the entire world. The Bishop then managed to have Barbarić transferred as Chaplain to Blagaj which is about 15 kilometres away from Medjugorje.

According to a testimony, it seems that Our Lady said to one of the visionaries that She wanted Father Slavko to remain in Medjugorje. I personally believe that it was true, otherwise he would not have been in Medjugorje for so long serving the pilgrims tirelessly against great odds ... such work requires superhuman physical strength. Father Slavko was a capable writer; he published his interviews with people from all over the world in the magazine «Sveta Baština» (Holy Heritage). These people, from all walks of life, talked about their spiritual experiences in Medjugorje.

He met, among others, a young princess Milona of Habsburg. She was fluent in six languages and a graduate with two degrees; she lived in Germany. Milona told how, after her first three days in Medjugorje, she changed so much that she could barely recognize herself. Milona felt a strong attraction towards Jesus and Mary wishing to merge with them she was sitting in the shade of the cross on Križevac Hill on the first day of her arrival. She felt herself becoming smaller and smaller and she felt the desire to be immersed in God. Here is her description:

"I was saying the rosary with everyone else and I felt strangely peaceful. But, at that moment while Our Lady appeared, I became very emotional and I commited myself to Her sincerely. I asked Her to remove all the sufferings and troubles that burdened my soul. I kept whispering: "Take everything, take everything!"

Then an incredible sensation of tenderness filled my being. I cannot describe it in words. All I know for sure is that from that moment I was free of burdens I had carried within me for many years. With the utmost joy I continued to repeat the invocation: "Cause of our joy' from the litany of Loreto.

For the first time in my life, I experienced true happiness. That day Our Lady removed great troubles from within me and I am convinced that She will do the same thing for whoever asks for Her help. From that day onwards I received new inner experiences which lead me closer and closer to God. If other young people, like me, come and appeal to Mother Mary here in Medjugorje, they will receive the answers to all their questions. She will show them how to find love, peace and tranquillity, for which man's heart longs from the depts of his soul. She will show them the direct path to Christ - the meaning of our being."

It was through Milona that her relatives of the Habsburg family, the Prince of Liechtenstein and many other noble families came to Medjugorje. They all accepted modest accommodation in the local houses and they were all happy there. The biggest favour Milona did for Medjugorje, however was her voluntary work: after having visited Medjugorje several times she offered Father Slavko her help in coordinating communications with the rest of the world.

Besides these noteworthy pilgrims who behaved modestly and graciously with the people of Medjugorje there were those who embarrassed the visionaries and the parishioners by bringing bags of worn clothing. A furclad lady gave a jumper with holes in it to my cousin in exchange for sleeping in her bed, free of charge! The visionaries asked Father Slavko what they were supposed to do with all the used clothing. He took out an old overcoat from a parcel that arrived from U.S.A., put it on and said: "Pity that the deceased was taller than I am!"

With his usual good humour the friar helped them overcome their embarrassment by explaining that many times wealthy people do not realize that helping others does not mean giving from our surplus, but sharing with others what we have and what we need. Just like the inhabitants of Medjugorje did, by sharing everything they had with the visitors during the first three years of the apparitions without worrying if they would have a piece of cheese or a drop of wine for the morrow. They lived like the widow described in the New Testament who gave everything she had and as a result Jesus said her gift was more valuable than the gifts from those who gave only what they did not need.

On 6th May, 1985 Ivanka, Ivan, Marija and Jakov had the apparition in the parish house. After only two minutes Marija, Jakov and Ivan whispered: "Ode!" (She's gone). Ivanka remained in ecstasy for a further six minutes. Marija was afraid because she did not understand what was happening to Ivanka; it was the first time she saw an apparition as an observer at the end of the apparition.

Ivanka said that she had received the tenth secret and that Our Lady had finished telling her the story about the future of humanity. The Queen of Peace also advised her to stay at home the next day and wait for her.

The Madonna stayed with Ivanka for one whole hour when She appeared the following day. This is how Ivanka described the apparition in her own words when she did eventually talk about it:

"Our Lady greeted me with: "Praised be Jesus", and I replied: "Praised be Jesus and Mary". She was with me a full hour. I've never seen Her look so beautiful. She was so tender and beautiful! She wore the most beautiful dress I have ever seen in my life. The dress sparkled like silver and gold. There were two angels with Her dressed in the same way as Our Lady. I cannot find words to describe their beauty. Such moments must be experienced to be understood.

Our Lady asked me what I would like and I replied: "To see my earthly Mother!". Our Lady smiled and nodded. My mother suddenly appeared wearing a grey gown. She was smiling. Our Lady told me to get up, so I did. My mother hugged me and kissed me saying: "My child, I'm so proud of you." Then she kissed me again and disappeared.

The Mother of Jesus continued, saying:

"My dear child, this is the last of our daily messages ... do not be sad. I shall come on every anniversary of the first apparition, the 25th June. Dear child, do not think that you have done anything wrong, that is not the reason why I shall come no more. No, it is not that, you have accepted and fostered the plans which my Son and I formulated for you completely, with all your heart. No one in the world has had the grace, which you, your brother and sister visionaries have received. Be happy because I am your Mother and I love you with all my heart. Ivanka, thank you because you answered my call and that of my Son. Thank you for persevering, for your patience in remaining with us while we needed you. Tell all your friends that my Son and I are always with you every-time that you need us."

I asked Our Lady if I could kiss Her and She nodded. I kissed Her. I asked Her to bless me. She smiled and then blessed me and said: "Go in peace with God" - and slowly went away, followed by the two angels.

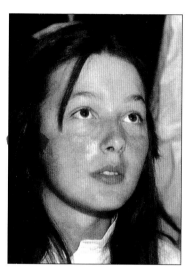 

Ivanka

Immediately after the apparition Ivanka ran to Vicka's home and there she cried and sobbed asking to be left alone. She was depressed for some days and asked that no one question her. Her father Ivan said that they felt as if a member of the family had gone when the apparitions stopped because they were all so accustomed to Our Lady.

Before Ivanka's apparitions had finished, she and the other visionaries were examined by a team of Italian doctors sponsored by the "Regina Pacis" association. After that, a second examination was carried out by French specialists, collaborators of the Medical Bureau for miraculous recoveries in Lourdes. Croatian doctors collaborated with the French.

Never before, in the history of the Church, were such sophisticated and detailed examinations ever carried out on visionaries. The detailed documentation of their works was submitted to the Vatican. Books have been written and videos made on the subject. Prof. René Laurentin (a famous expert on Mary), prof. Gildo Spaziante, author of "Studies for Medjugorje" and "The extraordinary healings", took part in the investigations along with the friars from Medjugorje.

Bishop Žanić showed no interest in these medical examinations nor did he order his committee to question any

From the left: doctor Mattalia, Marija, Jakov and Father Tomislav

doctors whom he trusted. One of his committee members, Father Nikola Bulat, arrived in the apparition room one day where such members rarely set foot. Here Father Bulat carried out test worthy of the Middle Ages: he stood behind Vicka with a big needle in his hand. He made the sign of the cross and then plunged it into her left shoulder blade.

Vicka was in a deep state of ecstasy and not a single muscle on her face contracted when the needle penetrated her. When she got up after the apparition, there was blood on her blouse.

The visionaries were not happy about these examinations at all. They told the Italian doctors that Our Lady had smiled in a goodnatured way at doctor Botta and the equipment he was using. When the visionaries asked Her what She thought about it, She replied that those things were not necessary. Doctor Botta was so deeply shaken that he immediately stopped any further tests.

When the French doctors came, after the Italians, Jakov refused to be examined saying that doctor Botta had given up doing any further tests. Later Jakov asked me if "my" Italian doctors still wanted to return to torment them. There was indeed that intention, shared by many others. In fact the tests on the visionaries still continue. Up to now no test or examination carried out at different times has ever raised any doubt as to the authenticity of the state of ecstasy of the visionaries.

I started writing my first book in the autumn of 1984. I was cautious, I did not speak about the difficulties imposed by the Communist Authorities because I knew that many books written by foreign authors who did, were seized at the borders. Father Laurentin was questioned because of his book as soon as he landed at the airport. Prof. Spaziante's book was confiscated from a group of forty-five Italians. In order to avoid problems of this kind, I limited myself to describing the first days of the apparitions and writing the testimonies of the inhabitants of Medjugorje and those of pilgrims from Italy, Austria and Germany, with whom I spoke personally.

My book includes the prayers that Jelena received from Our Lady through inner locution. This book was given away free at meetings organised by the Lecco group as evidence of the happenings at Medjugorje. I was sorry that the book was not written in Croatian, so I could have distribute it in my country. I always hoped that the time would come when I would be able to finance the Croatian edition and offer it to my people, who, even now, know less than the people abroad about the story of the apparitions.

It made me sad to think that the source of grace had chosen my country, but my people, although thirsting for God, could not drink from that very fountain. To make up for this, I sent copies of the prayers Jelena received on 22nd June 1985 to all my friends and relatives in Croatia urging them to make photocopies of them and to distribute the prayers to all those who wished to read them. Here are the contents of those prayers:

"Oh, my God, behold this sick person before You. He has come to ask You what he desires and what he considers as the most important thing for him. You, oh my God, make my heart understand that the health of the soul is the most important thing: Lord, may Your Holy Will be done in everything. If You want him to be cured, let health be given to him; but if Your Will is different, let him continue to bear his cross. I also pray to You for us, who intercede for him; purify our hearts, to make us worthy to convey Your Holy

Mercy. Protect him and relieve his pain. That Your Holy Will shall be done in him, that Your Holy Name be glorified through him. Help him to bear his cross with courage.

(Then a Glory Be is recited three times)

"Oh, God, our hearts are in darkness, in spite of our link to your heart. Our hearts struggle between You and satan; do not permit it to be like that! Every time our hearts are divided between good and evil let them be enlightened by Your light and let them be united. Never allow that there be two loves; that two faiths ever coexist in us and that love and hatred, honesty and dishonesty, humility and pride do not coexist.

Help us, on the contrary, so that our hearts may be reised to You just like the heart of a childern. May our hearts be captivated by Your peace and always long for it. May Your Holy Will and Your love dwell in us and that at least sometimes we really wish to be Your children and help us to receive You again. We open our hearts to You so that Your Will dwell in us. We open our souls to You so that they may be touched by Your Holy Mercy which will help us to see all our sins, and will help us to realise that that which makes us impure is sin.

God, we want to be Your humble and devoted children, to the point of becoming Your cherished and sincere children, as You our Father would desire us to be. Help us, Jesus, our brother, to obtain the forgiveness of the Father and help us to be good towards Him. Help us, Jesus, to understand clearly what God gives us because sometimes we give up doing a good deed believing it to be a wrong"

(Recite three Glory Be at the end)

My efforts with the book and other obligations did not allow me to return to Medjugorje as soon as I would have liked. At the beginning of the summer of 1985, a girl from Zagreb called me. An Italian priest had baptized her in India. She arrived in Medjugorje and wanted to receive the sacrament of Confirmation. She called Father Slavko who said that he needed her baptismal certificate. This was why the girl, Carmen, asked me to contact the priest in Modena who had baptized her. She also asked me to be her godmother. I replied that I would be glad to, but that I would not be going to Medjugorje before August.

Several days later, her mother Zdenka called me and asked me if I could arrive for 7th July. I promised her that I would do my best. The date was getting closer but the certificate from Modena was late in arriving. Inexplicably the express-registered letter with document was "lost" in the postman's letter bag for four long days. On discovering this delay, I got very angry: I had to telephone Carmen and advise her to postpone the ceremony that I could not be there on time with her baptismal certificate.

In the meantime, her mother Zdenka had also decided to receive the sacrament of Confirmation and she chose the visionary Marija as her godmother. Before leaving I asked myself what I should wear and decided on packing a plain white dress. On arrival in Medjugorje I discovered that all four of us, unknown to each other, had chosen a white dress. Father Slavko told us that Bishop Žanić had promised to officiate at the Confirmation but Slavko was not at all sure that he would keep his promise. I had only one day to ensure that mother and daughter had learned everything necessary for Confirmation since I was afraid that the Bishop might catch them out on some point of doctrine.

There was a group from Mexico attending Mass on the day I arrived. They had brought a sacred vestment with an image of Our Lady of Guadalupe on it for the priest.

On the day planned for the Confirmation, 13th July, the visionary Marija, head bowed and in a hurry, met us just under the stairs leading to the clergy house. As she mounted the stairs she casually looked down at the crowd below and saw a priest, she asked Father Slavko to invite the priest up, to the room.

Father Slavko did so and was very surprised to discover that the priest was none other than the Bishop of Warsaw! Father Slavko was quick to ask the Bishop if he would be willing to confirm the mother and daughter as it was clear that the Bishop of Mostar would not be coming for the ceremony. The Bishop agreed and was given the sacred vestment, from Mexico, to wear.

I stood near the altar, with my back to the crowd, Carmen was next to me, then there was her mother Zdenka and in a corner away from curious eyes was the visionary Marija. We had to protect her from the pushing congregation who might easily have knocked her down from the altar.

All four of us were extremely happy. During the Mass and the Confirmation rites, we felt such a great love pouring into us. Two foreign journalists, one German the other Italian, invited by Zdenka, felt the same way about it.

After the Confirmation I waited for the Bishop outside the church. I approached him and thanked him, in Italian, for having confirmed my godchild. He was visibly touched and asked me who the two were. I answered: "A famous communist journalist and her daughter". The next day all four of us went to the parish office to sign the confirmation certificate. Father Slavko showed us the Polish Bishop's visiting card and said: "I had no time to read his name yesterday: it's Mons. Jozef Zbiegniew Kraszewski".

At the time, none of us knew that this Bishop was a good friend of Pope Wojtila and that he was going to visit the Pope directly from Medjugorje. About ten days later, the Czech Bishop Hnilica, who was in exile, arrived on a private visit accompanied by the Pope's good frind Wanda Poltawska. (When the Pope was a young priest, he wrote a letter to Father Pio to beg him to pray for Poltawska, mother of four children and seriously ill with cancer. The lady was healed. It is said that when the young Wojtila returned to thank Father Pio, the Friar kneeled before him perhaps aware that he was in the presence of the future Pope).

From the right: Mons. Kraszewski, the author, Carmen, Father Slavko, Zdenka; behind them, hidden, the visionary Marija

Only then did I realize that there had been no reason to be angry with the postman; if he had given me the letter on time, Bishop Kraszewski would not have confirmed Carmen and her mother. He would have come incognito and left incognito.

This event made me realize how we often try to force things to happen instead of trusting in Divine Providence.

After the apparition and Holy Mass, the visionaries usually went home and recited the glorious mysteries of the rosary. After that, they would take the Holy Writ and contemplate the passage they read.

On one occasion, the Magnificat (My soul magnifies the Lord) caught Ivan's attention.

They felt that they had to recite it after the apparition and they have done so ever since, because it was the prayer of gratitude of the Blessed Virgin.

Vicka was always in very great pain which hardly ever left her so she had the apparitions alone. She did not complain, she carried the burden with a smile. Her family got used to her condition and accepted the fact that she would never ask the Virgin for relief. They assumed that her suffering was a part of God's plan for her.

Mirjana kept praying for those who ignored God and she inspired other people to do the same. Ivan and his prayer group often went to Podbrdo Hill at night to pray for the intentions of Our Lady.

The entire group of young people grew with him through prayer. Sometimes when the pilgrims heard that Ivan was going to the mountain, they would accompany him in their hundreds.

Jakov prayed for the sick, the pilgrims and sinners. His father had died a year after his mother, so now that he was alone; his mother's relatives took care of him.

In the meantime Father Jozo had become the Parish Priest of Tihaljina which is very near Medjugorje. The Italians were happy about this because it meant they could visit him. Group after group went to see him and he preached in Italian, which he had learned in prison. They absorbed and taped his every sermon and meditation. They made transcriptions and distributed them to the people at home.

While Father Jozo was praying over them many pilgrims would fall to the ground "resting in the spirit". On one occasion, when I was with an Italian group, I met an old lady who was keeping house for the friar. She confided that he ate next to nothing, neglected the house, and she lamented it was difficult to live with a "saint".

In the meantime Father Tomislav Vlašić completely withdrew into prayer, he even asked his superiors to relieve him from all duties in order to better follow the call of Our Lady. A group of young people from the prayer group, inspired by Jelena, gathered around him. Marija was with them, also.

They lived a life of prayer and seclusion in order to see if this would be their future vocation. Jelena and Marijana could not join them because they had to go to school. They continued to guide the prayer group which, although now smaller, met regularly once a week near the parish house.

It was at this point that Father Slavko became the central figure in the parish. He continually fed the pilgrims with information in Italian, German, French and, with the help of Milona, also the English speaking pilgrims. He often led the worship and the prayers for the sick. He continued to pray on Podbrdo Hill and on Križevac. At the same time, he attended to his official duties in the parishes where he was assigned. He took care of the visionaries to the best of his ability, including both Jelena and Marijana.

Father Josip Bubalo, a poet, was always with him in the parish. He had taped his long conversation with Vicka and wrote an interesting book about it called: 'A thousand meetings with Our Lady'.

The third friar of the trio was Father Stanko Vasilj, who, as I mentioned before, tirelessly led the singing in the church until he became seriously ill and had to retire to a monastery.

By the end of 1986, on the Feast of the Holy Family, the visionary Ivanka married Rajko Elez, who was from one of the poorest Medjugorje families. The enemies of Medjugorje tried to use this by insinuating that clearly the apparitions were only a farce.

Many, however, defended the visionary claiming that marriage is a sacrament, and that today when the family institution is in danger, there is great need to give the example of a true Christian family.

After the marriage Ivanka retired to private life. She lives in Medjugorje and, while I write, is the mother of three children, Kristina, Josip and Ivan.

Not only Ivanka, but also the other visionaries have also grown into mature and responsible young people. They do their best to help the visiting pilgrims to establish prayer groups in their hometowns like those in Medjugorje.

What the Croatians first experienced at the beginning of the apparitions is now being experienced by other nations ... one after the other following some kind of unwritten "plan", they continue to arrive at Medjugorje, first the Austrians and Italians, then the French, Americans and Japanese.

They, too, have witnessed hundreds of miraculous recoveries, as can be read in the Parish Chronicle.

I will mention only two:

Diana Basile from Milan instantly recovered from multiple sclerosis after she came to Medjugorje, Rita Klaus from America recovered from the same illness.

Both were considered incurable by doctors.

Ivanka's marriage

Invitations to the visionaries to visit Austria, Italy, Germany, France, Australia, and America were increasingly frequent. They accepted and wherever they went they continued to have their apparitions. This too is the proof that Our Lady has come to awaken the people all over the world. Ivan after having abandoned the seminary, visited his relatives in America and testified there. This withdrawn and shy young man has turned out to be a brave messenger of Our Lady. Jakov was invited to Switzerland, with great success. Vicka and a friend went to Lourdes, she had an apparition there thus privately "renewing" the apparition of Our Lady in that famous sanctuary.

Marija, in the meantime, had realized that she could not spread the messages of Our Lady by living in isolation so she left Father Tomislav's community to dedicate herself totally to the pilgrims.

She was invited to Fatima. The visionary and her companions travelled trough different cities and stopped every day in different churches to pray and to allow Marija to have her daily appointment with Our Lady.

On their way through Spain, one evening as the time of the apparition was getting nearer, they could not find a church. So they pulled off the road and stopped in a meadow. They got out of the car and kneeled by Marija who, on that occasion, had a particularly long apparition. At the end of it she recited the Magnificat as usual and it was only then that she realized that she heard mooing around her. She was alone and surrounded by bulls, while her friends had quietly made their way back to their car during the apparition. She knew that prayer alone could save her. She did not move, she just prayed. And the bulls went away, one by one. That's why Our Lady was smiling so mysteriously during the apparition, she said to her self!

Marija also lived through another harrowing situation: her brother Andrija had a kidney disease and needed regular dialysis. His only chance or survival was a kidney transplant. Marija generously volunteered as the donor.

An American professor, who visited Medjugorje as a pilgrim, offered to perform this complicated surgery. Mother Iva was desperate for she was afraid she would lose both daughter and son. Just before the operation, Marija asked the Holy Mother to assist Her.

While entering the operating theatre she joked with the surgeon asking him to give her a strong dose of anaesthesia because if the Holy Mother were to appear she was sure to jump down from the operating table and kneel in prayer!

Our Lady actually did appear and stayed with her during the operation. Marija knew what was happening to her by the expression on the Virgin's face.

After this major surgery, Marija went to Italy for her convalescence, she stayed with friends. The pilgrims would never have left her in peace at home and she needed all the rest possible.

By now she was playing a vital role in Medjugorje: the Holy Mother continued to entrust her with messages for the parish every Thursday and ... as of 25th January 1987, the Feast of St. Paul's conversion, She extended these messages to the entire world every 25th day of each month.

Father Slavko was always in touch with Marija; he received the monthly message from her which he translated, with the help of his collaborators, into many languages. Every month he commented on Our Lady's message and followed her suggestions together with many people from all over the world. Inspired by these extraordinary messages Don Mario Galbiati, from a small town in Italy called Erba, founded Radio Maria. Now his broadcasting reaches out all over the world: his programmes are in different languages and include the recitation of the rosary or live Mass from different churches. Radio Maria is now managed by Father Livio Fanzaga

Father Slavko and Father Mario on Radio Maria

while Don Mario also founded Radio Mater, another broadcasting station. Both have a large following ... day and night ... and not only by the disabled and elderly.

Another priest, Angelo Mutti, started a bulletin in Mantova called the "Echo of Medjugorje", which was soon published in many languages. "Gebetsaktion" (The action of Prayer) was founded in Vienna while in Turin the magazine "Medjugorje" was produced among many others that were started spontaneously by the pilgrims. Countless videos and books in various languages have been produced too.

The TV Ljubljana made a good film about the apparitions, and immediately afterwards another one was made by the Belgrade state television which was also quite good. Perhaps these very films contributed to the fact that, after that, the Communist Authorities gradually stopped harassing the visionaries and friars.

However, difficulties and obstacles have always occurred. Bishop Žanić requested that Catholic priests all over the world, should be prevented from accompanying pilgrims officially. The Bishop was on the point of making an official declaration against the apparitions, so he crossed the Adriatic Sea on the way to Rome to meet Cardinal Ratzinger, who was head of the Congregation of the Doctrine of the Faith. In Rome Žanić was surprised to learn that the Cardinal had relieved him of his specific responsibilities and requested that the Episcopal Conference of Yugoslavia establish a new committee to access the apparitions.

The Bishop's negative attitude had not discouraged other bishops and cardinals, mostly in incognito, to become pilgrims to Medjugorje. They came from all over the world. Many laymen who had never organized visits to sanctuaries, volunteered as guides for the pilgrims: Darija Škunca from Canada, has been guiding groups for years. Wayne Weible, an ex-protestant, inflamed the interest of Americans by his testimonies; every year he organizes charter flights to Medjugorje. Alberto Bonifacio, Maria Naggi and many others bring Italians to Medjugorje every month.

Because of this enormous participation of people from all over, some of the fierce opposers insinuated that the friars had invented everything themselves, to make money out of the situation. To which Father Slavko calmly replied:

"I'm really sorry but we friars are certainly not so powerful! Not one of us invested a single penny in propaganda. We haven't got a team of managers to place the messages. It was the Holy Mother who found Her own collaborators. Everything that happens here is Her work. The friars didn't call anyone ... It's Our Lady who calls the people. What the friars, visionaries and parish do is to host, as best they can, those who come. What is more, the pilgrims no longer arrive here searching for information. Now they request formation, they want spiritual growth and this imposes an even greater responsibility on us."

So many people arrive daily at Medjugorje that the one-time hamlet has changed completely. Tourist agencies have been established encouraging the building of hotels. Souvenir sellers have sprung up ten-a-penny, conducted by wily tradesmen, mostly from Italy, where they have long experience in the field. As I mentioned earlier, the Medjugorje parishioners did not want any trade whatsoever, they believed that it was wrong to sell holy objects, etc. and very reluctantly charged for food and lodging. When they did, they included wine, grappa and coffee with meals offering a lot for the little they asked. Many still host poor people free of charge to this day.

Once, when I was in Medjugorje with a group, I had the privilege of being with Father Ettore who keeps a house for the homeless at Seregno, Italy. On our return he told us of how, a few months before, in Milan Central Station they had found someone who did not want to move from a stone bench. When they eventually managed to convince him to move, they discovered, with horror, that the soles of his feet were rotting. I was still under shock after hearing this terrible story when one of the ladies travelling with us complained that in the families in Medjugorje all the food was served on the same plate. I took a deep breath and then replied: "My dear lady, the purpose of this pilgrimage was to spend a few days with the families; pray with them and listen to the messages. The expenses of the trip go mostly to the bus company and only a small part goes to those who hosted us and unfortunately, there are still some who are so poor that they cannot afford to buy plates for starters, salad, dessert."

I thought to myself: 'This is what's happening to the people of Medjugorje, obliged to become professional caterers, they will neglect the fields, get rid of their animals because their smell bothers the pilgrims more every day. They will no longer cultivate tobacco; they'll have to take out mortgages so they can build houses which will then have to be rebuilt because they no longer suit the demands of the Travel-Agencies, who ask for places to sleep for 50 people in the same house. Those who have small houses will stay poor!'

I also asked myself if the villagers would manage to preserve all the grace they had received in the new circumstances or would they be trapped by a new style of life? I remembered how the Madonna had warned that satan wanted to destroy Her work. Now was the moment: those people, who, until yesterday, had been happy with their lot, were now in danger of neglecting their prayers and their spiritual life in the race for material gains. Moreover, the village no longer belonged to them. The competition arrives from outside and imposes accelerated rhythms of life which inexorably change their beautiful patriarchal way of living perhaps causing them to drift away from each other.

There is a real danger that in only ten years time the same thing will happen to Medjugorje as has happened in Lombardy, Italy, where I live. One hundred years ago the people here were much closer to each other, united, they helped one another and worked together in the fields. In the evenings they would recite the rosary. Nowadays factories lie on those very fields ... everyone thinks only of himself ... neighbours are strangers. To avoid this I think that the inhabitants of Medjugorje must remain devoted to the messages of Our Lady.

Our Lady's School

The visionaries were the first to have their lives completely changed. Sister Elvira, who has devoted all her life to drug addicts, visited Marija. Marija's relatives allowed her to set a tent on their ground for her group from Italy. Sister Elvira was a very practical woman and she soon realised the difficult situation in which Marija's family found themselves. Together with her young group she had a bathroom built on to the house; the same for the houses of the other visionaries ... and, in doing so, the old style of houses began to change.

Despite their great popularity, the six visionaries from Medjugorje remained humble and modest. Ivan did not complete his education at the seminary. He did his military service in Ljubljana and he continued to have his visions at his friend's house while he was off duty. Jakov graduated from the Polytechnic. Vicka was at the pilgrims' disposal all the time even though she was not very well physically. After the surgery, Marija experienced health problems and often had to go to hospital for tests and medical care. Mirjana graduated in agriculture.

Our Lady chose the children to help Her in teaching the adults. The American president Bush received the visionary Ivan. After listening carefully to what Ivan had to say Bush said that he then knew exactly what he was going to say to the Russian President Gorbachev. An Italian politician, asked Marija's advice regarding his politics and personal life.

In spite of meetings with other famous people too, they remained untouched and they endeavoured to live their lives in compliance with God's will. They did not yield during difficulties and remained faithful to the promises they had made as young children: "I see Our Lady and it is through me that She invites all of us to peace." Over the many long years of apparitions many of those who have met the visionaries have had unrelistic expectations.They do not understand that the visionaries are people like you and me who must make every effort so as not to stray from the path of holiness.

Like them, we too are requested to attend Our Lady's school of peace. To live in peace means to love, forgive and be compassionate towards everyone and everything. It is a very difficult school. The Virgin Mary knows this well; perhaps this is why the apparitions have lasted so long. Vicka is an excellent student of this school. She does not spare herself: every day, when she is at home winter or summer, she speaks from the balcony to the people standing in the yard with such love and wisdom. These are her words:

"Who can claim to be converted nowadays? No one. He who says so probably lies. He, who says he wants to convert,

Father Slavko, the last on the right, leads the Way of the Cross

is on the path of conversion, he prays for his conversion. I know that I can live Our Lady's messages better than I am doing, so I urge myself to do better every day. Others too, know that they can do better. They can do it! Nowadays everything is hurry, hurry, hurry. Where are we hurring to? We should never say "I must, I must!" God's will is in everything, we can do everything. We create the rythm, the tempo. If we were to say "slow down", then the world would change too! The most important thing to do is to start changing within, changing our hearts."

In the spring of 1989, Ivanka Vana Jakić arrived from America. In the course of her conversation with Father Leonard Oreč, then Pastor of Medjugorje, the former Pastor Father Tomislav Vlašić and Vesna Krmpotić, a great idea was conceived - to establish Medjugorje as a "Peace Zone" on the level of the United Nations. Vana took responsibility of organising the project and she asked for the support of many secular and religious authorities in the U.S.A. and in Bosnia.

All of them endorsed documents in favour of Medjugorje. Following that, Vana successfully met with Cattolics, Muslims, Orthodox Christians and Jews representatives presenting them with her plan to declare Medjugorje officially "Peace Zone" along with seven other places common to other religions in Bosnia. She was fully aware that she was only carrying out the Holy Mother's grand initiative, and was tireless and unwavering in establishing the first eight Republic Zones of Peace in Former Bosnia and Hercegovina. Undoubtedly, that was clear evidence of the divine intervention of the Holy Mother just before the outbreak of the war in the former Yugoslavia.

Then Vana went to India, where she met with Mother Teresa of Calcutta who gave her written support for "World Centres of Prayer for Peace". The saintly lady approved adding that she would have gladly visited Medjugorje but she was afraid it would draw too much attention to herself. The Dalai Lama, himself a Nobel Peace Prize winner, also listened with great attention while Vana told him about the apparitions in Medjugorje. The Dalai Lama was obviously fully aware that such an initiative for peace in that area of the world was of the utmost importance. He too, endorsed the project. Returning from India Vana went to Italy and there, in the Vatican, she met Pope John Paul II who gave his blessing to the project of Christian Peace Zones, including Jerusalem. Then she met with Father Massimiliano Mizzi OFM Conv., Delegate General for Ecumenism and Inter-religious Dialogue of the International Franciscan Center for Dialogue at Assisi. He, too, responded enthusiastically to the idea of protected, sacred places.

Although Sister Elvira was unaware of Vana's idea, she used to say that Medjugorje was a real zone of peace, where she found it easier to work with drug addicts than in Italy. Here, under Our Lady's heavenly protection, these restless young people, destroyed by drugs, became calm, peaceful, and happy. Elvira's group initiated the first youth festival organized by Father Slavko which saw the participation of many young people from many countries.

Everyone showed interest in sister Elvira's method of curing the drug addicts. She patiently explained that it was the Holy Mother's method not hers and it consisted in: "Prayers ... prayers and more prayers!". When a youth discovers the value of prayer he comes to know Christ through it and no longer needs drugs.

My friends told me how wonderful that first youth festival was. I was unable to attend as my mother-in-law suffered another severe stroke and I did my best to assist sher overestimating my own strength. I fell ill physically and

238

Father Slavko and Vicka lead the March for Peace

A view of Medjugorje: "Peace Zone"

psycologically. My being so worn-out caused me to forget what I had learned at Our Lady's school. I forgot to abandon my problems and worries ... leaving them to Jesus. I allowed myself to be overcome by every day difficulties, I failed my first important spiritual exam. But I resolved to pass it second time round ... when it came! I prepared myself carefully thankful to the Virgin Mary that my daughter's health allowed her to attend school regularily. I told myself to be patient that sooner or later I would return to Medjugorje. I was unaware that years would pass before I could return.

In September 1989 the visionary Mirjana married her childhood suitor, Marko Soldo, nephew of Father Slavko. Marko had given up hope of marrying her when she had her visions. However, his dreams came true, for it was obviously in the Lord's plans that they should wed. Mirjana never ever said she would go into a convent, she always expressed a wish to dedicate her life to having a family and praying for those who deny God's existence.

Every year on 18th March, on her birthday, the Virgin appears to her; Our Lady speaks about the secrets, so that sometimes immediately after the apparition she cries and withdraws to the solitude of her room. Although this annual vision occurs on her birthday, Mirjana has explained that this date has another meaning to it and has nothing to do with her birthday. We will know, when the time is right, just why She has chosen the 18th March.

The War

On the tenth anniversary of the apparitions, 25th June, 1991, approximately one hundred and fifty thousand pilgrims arrived in Medjugorje. Dreadful news disrupted the joyful prayers and singing of these people, war had broken out: the Yugoslav army had bombed Ljubljana the capital of Slovenia. On that tragic day, Our Lady gave the following message:

"Dear children, today on this great day that you have given to me, I wish to bless all of you and say that these days, while I am with you, are days of grace. My desire is to teach you and to help you walk the path of holiness. There are many people who do not want to listen to my messages and accept what I say seriously. This is why I invite you and pray that your daily lives are a testimony of my presence. Pray and God will help you discover the true reason for my coming. Therefore children, pray and read the Sacred Scriptures so that through my coming you may discover their message for you. Thank you for answering my call."

The pilgrims went home by land through Croatia. At Knin they met with the first road barricades. It was the beginning of the war; the country was attacked by the federal army. Recruits from all of the six Yugoslav Republics were in the barracks there while their mothers surrounded these barracks and bravely asked the generals to let their children return home; they did not want them forced to shoot their own people. Those young soldiers who managed to escape from the army went abroad. They were considered deserters. Those who came to Italy were Catholics, Orthodox, Muslims and atheists.

The Yugoslav Federal Army, one of the strongest in Europe, attacked Croatia and started bombing city after city. Their favorite targets were Catholic churches. They shelled them so heavily that only heaps of stones remained. The army generals were mainly Serbian communists whose aim was to prevent Croatia from becoming an independent state. The Croatians had to flee in their thousands from the bombed cities of Vukovar, Osijek, S. Brod, Zadar, Gospić... They arrived in Rijeka, which was not so safe either, because war ships were anchored in Kvarner Bay.

Realising how serious the situation was, I tried in vain to organise help. People did not understand. No wonder! Italian television and press relayed news from Belgrade sources which blamed the Croatians for the war. The Italians did not understand the real circumstances, even after the Vatican openly favoured the independence of Croatia.

In the end I managed to find an organisation of volunteers willing to help, with them I managed to collect enough basic necessities to be able to leave for Rijeka where I found refugees accommodated in the hotels in Opatija, Lovran and areas nearby. I will never forget an old woman there, dressed in black, a scarf around her head from which wisps of white hair tried to escape. Her face was wrinkled, her eyes stared, lost, bewildered. She was standing at the hotel entrance and, above the door, there was the hotel name written in gold letters: "Excelsior".

A year later war broke out in Bosnia. There was a new wave of refugees arriving in Rijeka where the hotels were already full. There was no available accommodation so they were sent to the schools in nearby villages.

Once, on arriving with one of many trucks full of supplies, I met a lady, Vesna from Sarajevo. She was crying. I told her to calm down and be patient that God sees and fore-

Some obsessed soldiers even shot at Crucifix

sees everything. I explained that I, too, was a refugee as a child, and here I was back helping them. At first she looked puzzled then she managed a smile to let me know she understood what I was trying to explain to her. Vesna was with her ten-year-old daughter Ivana who was upset because they had no news from her father, Vesna's husband, who was in Sarajevo:

"Dear Ivana", I suggested. "Before you go to sleep tonight, pray to your guardian angel. Tell him to contact your daddy's guardian angel, then to go together to Jesus and ask Him to protect your daddy and find a way of giving you his news. Neither you or your mummy can go to Sarajevo but your guardian angel can. He will spread his beautiful wings and fly above those mad people who have been shelling our hometown."

Two days later Ivana's father managed to call a relative in Rijeka, via satellite, through the UN peacekeeping forces. Little Ivana's prayer had worked!

On another occasion in Rijeka I met up with Alberto Bonifacio leading a convoy of supplies to Medjugorje. I asked him to give my love to my relatives and friends; that I was sorry I could not go with him, but I was needed at Rijeka as there were thousands of refugees and very few volunteers to help them.

The French Lay Sister Emmanuel of the Beatitudes stayed in Medjugorje during the war. She continued to relay Our Lady's messages to the prayer groups around the world and she did her best to explain the real situation of the war to her fellow contrymen in France. Lay Sister Emmanuel asked Vicka how she felt about the Serbs and if she prayed for them. She replied:

"Of course I do. When Our Lady tells us to pray She means us to pray for all the people. We must pray for the

Serbian people, regardless of all the sufferings they have caused. If we cannot love them and forgive them, this war will never end. The important thing for us to do is not to think of revenge. We must say: "Thank you God for all the pain and trouble you have given to our people and we pray for those Serbs who do not know what are they doing. There are people among us who do not love the Serbs and who would like them as far away as possible from us.

We must instead wish them well, we must pray for them, for our prayer can touch their hearts and make them realise that this war is not good for anybody. Our Lady has often told us that war is satan's doing. Satan is so powerful that he influences our thoughts in every possible way. He has now attacked us viciously so we must take care of our thoughts."

The visionary Marija was also in Medjugorje during the war. She contemplated on the messages of peace that Our Lady had given them right from very beginning of the apparitions and then on the new ones where the Holy Mother had warned that they were walking the lost path of pain and suffering; that She had prayed with them for ten long years in order to prevent this bloodshed.

Jakov was calledup by the army to be recruited and trained to kill his own people. He escaped to Italy where he and his Italian friends organized aid and supplies for his country. Ivan did not join the war. His fellow countrymen told him to stay at home and pray for them. Pilgrims from America contacted him frequently increasing their prayers and fasting for peace.

Mirjana and Ivanka also remained in Medjugorje.

In the meantime, Father Jozo was transferred to a monastery in Široki Brijeg. He comforted the soldiers who were going to fight. Bombs exploded around the convent, killing several people in their homes. His nephew was killed fighting. Pilgrims still arrived despite the war and when they enquired why there was a war right there Fr. Jozo replied:

"The war did not start here, it started in Heaven on Earth. This is where the great war against communism ends. It is the confirmation of the profecy of Fatima about the conversion of Russia and the defeat of the atheist system that was introduced here. This is the start of a new beginning where the pure heart of Mary will triumph through the conversion of people and the birth of a new mentality which will create a better future. In these times of war we see the hearts of men so chained to evil that they even kill members of their own family if they differ in opinion. It is through Our Lady that God has created this oasis of peace. This war is purifying this oasis from the roots of evil."

When they asked Friar Jozo if this was a war of religions he replied:

"Nobody can say that Hitler was a Catholic or a Protestant. Neither can we say that the Serbian generals are Orthodox. These are people who are in the hands of satan whose only desire is to retain their power and drag the people down with them. Our Lady does not request the United Nations to send soldiers to help because it is well known that no army can create harmony, stability or peace. Peace is, above all, a gift from God which comes to us only through prayer. It is a gift which flows from a forgiving heart. Satan can be beaten only by prayer and fasting. I beg of you all to pray and fast for us. Thank you for helping us maintain this Oasis of Peace."

The seventy-four year old Bishop Žanić managed to escape into the street just a few minutes before his house was hit by a bomb. Everybody in Medjugorje was happy his life was saved, even if he had publically expressed his hope that

Monsignor Ratko Perić would succeed him when he, Žanić, retired. Perić, like Žanić, strongly opposed the apparitions in Medjugorje.

While the Mostar parks were transformed into cemeteries, Serb bombers flew over Medjugorje ready to drop their bombs. However, everytime they were above the village a strange light blinded the pilots preventing them from taking any kind of action.

The men from Medjugorje were hiding in the hills among the bramble bushes ready to defend their village if need be. Each one of them wore a rosary around his neck which was blessed by the Holy Mother.

Thousands of refugees found shelter in Medjugorje. The Mass was held in the basement of the clergy house and it was there, in 1992, that the hundred years' celebration of the parish took place. Water and electricity were scarce. Seventy percent of the women and children had left the village.

The shops were empty and closed; the Podrbo Hill and Križevac Hill were deserted, nobody climbed them. It looked as if satan had won. Our Lady appeared to Ivan every evening and, through him, comforted "Her children".

Volunteers from Italy, France, Austria and Germany supplied aid. They became a connection between Medjugorje and the people who prayed and fasted abroad for the end of the war. It was through them that the messages of Our Lady circulated through the world. Pilgrims were eager to hear the messages every 25th day of the month.

Messages in Croatian reached the prayer groups in Belgrade and Novi Sad, established by the Orthodox, through their foreign prayer centers. When I heard this I was pleased for my people who prayed and relied on God. They even had support from the enemy side! This goes to show that Our

Lady does not exclude anybody from Her plan for saving the world. Those who were willing to pray for Her intention had the opportunity to do so, from both sides of the barricades.

Ivan and Vicka said that the war was not a part of the secrets, that Our Lady was sad and that She prayed with them for peace to come as soon as possible. Our Lady acted the same way as when Jesus was tortured: She prayed then, too, She did not write petitions to the Jews and Romans asking them to set Her Son free. It is through this example that Our Lady teaches us how to pray and how to surrender ourselves to the Lord's Will, even when our situations, as people or nations, seem to be so difficult and dangerous.

While the war was raging, the visionary Marija returned from South America, where she had been on a mission with Father Slavko. She caught such a serious infection there that she could not stand the pain. She accepted to suffer until Easter and she prayed to God to release her from her sufferance on that day. Her brothers were with the army at the front where they confessed regularily fully aware that anything could happen and wishing to be in God's grace all the time. In this, Marija saw the better side of the war.

The war continued to rage: bombs fell on the hills, bombs fell on the outskirts of the village but none fell on the houses or the church which were important targets. A young boy from Medjugorje was killed in Mostar. He was not as lucky as the others hidden among the brambles or in the mud on the surrounding hills. While the bullets whistled round their heads they recited one Hail Mary after another ... and were lucky enough not be wounded. Vicka's brothers survived the terrible part of the war too.

Foreigners who lived in Medjugorje during the war sent faxes home in which they stated that the population of Medjugorje prayed more for the Serbs than for the Croatians. It was well known that the Serbian soldiers were treated harshly: they were forced to the front and if they refused they were shot. They were drugged, a fact confirmed by Serbian soldier who was recovering in hospital in Split.

Father Slavko who, as a psychologist, knew just how strong and destructive hate could be, encouraged the parishioners to offer prayers and a the novena to the Holy Spirit for the enemy. He particularly insisted on fasting too. He prayed for all the friends of Medjugorje, all over the world, requesting them to fast and repent for this reason and create a chain of love that would repel satan and his servants.

In full swing of the war, Pope John Paul II received the visionary Marija in private. Nobody knows what was said.

Jakov and Father Jozo also went after her. During the general meeting, on a Wednesday, they stood in the first row among the people waiting for His Holiness. When the Pope approached Jakov, the latter stretched out his hand but a strange woman pulled at the Pope's tunic and, while the guards took her away, the Pope moved on.

Then he arrived in front of Father Jozo who, while stretching out his hand, explained that he was from Medjugorje. The Pope smiled kindly and said:

"Medjugorje, yes I know. Medjugorje...Defend Medjugorje! I am with you. I bless you all. Be brave, I am with you. Support Medjugorje! Convey my greeting to everybody and tell them that I know about your sufferings in this war."

During a sermon delivered in Medjugorje, Father Jozo talked about the massacre of approximately one hundred children. He said:

"We abhor this murder of one hundred children, killed by wars, but we do not abhor, nor do we cry, for the children killed in their mother's womb. What difference is there between the generals who order the killings of people in towns and villages and those parents who condemn their unborn children to death? How can we pray to God to protect our youth if we, ourselves, kill these innocent souls? How many innocent children died in our towns before the Serbs started the war? Let us reflect on this and remember what Our Lady has been repeating for years: "Convert, abandon sin!"

On one occasion, the visionary Ivan commented the war: "I personally suffer, with my people, through this war. I constantly pray that it will end soon. I suffer because the world lacks understanding; because those in power seem to have misunderstood the real reasons which have caused the war. Many do not understand that this is a war between darkness and light, between good and evil. Our Lady said so in Her messages. The war has not induced any doubts in me. It has strengthened my faith and inspired me to contribute to its end through prayer. Our Lady asks this of me too."

When the foreign pilgrims asked Father Slavko why Europe and America did not stop the concentration camps in Bosnia, he replied:

"If a nation is used to the idea that thousands of its young people die daily from drugs and thousands of innocent

From the left: Marija, Milona and Father Slavko

babies are killed through abortions, why should it bother to help avoid the massacre of five thousand Croatians and ten thousand Muslims? Destruction and war are rooted in utter contempt for life. Peace depends on our conversion to life ... our love for life ... our determination to defend life right from the beginning, in the mother's womb!"

The second phase of the war was even more terrible that the first: the Croatians and Muslims, who were allies at first, became enemies. The Serbian generals took advantage by overturning the situation, thus weakening both armies defending the territory. Their quarrel gave them the excuse to intervene and realize their goals for a greater Serbia. This gave Europe, and the world, a good excuse to give even less aid to the people. The Italian press and TV reported it on terms as if it were some kind of pub quarrel or, at the most, a sort of tribal war of which everyone was equally responsible.

251

Their attitude changed to "let them get on with it ... between themselves!". We, who collected aid, were quick to realize the change of heart in the people who now held a different opinion about the war in Bosnia and no longer responded spontaneously to our appeals for help.

In the midst of these sad events, something lovely happened: Jakov, twenty-two, married the Italian Annalisa Barozzi at Easter 1993. Now Jakov, too, had a family again, and a good wife who had been a frequent pilgrim to Medjugorje. Nowadays young couples struggle to decide whether to marry or not. To avoid the responsibilities of marriage they follow the dubious examples of film stars and TV personalities who change their "live-in" partners almost as frequently as their clothes. Christian weddings are still a valid reality, a corner stone for society. With their marriages, the visionaries have been given the opportunity to inspire the world to return to the way of life as God determined when he created man and woman.

Sad news also arrived: another young man from Medjugorje was killed and another was seriously wounded. Three Italian volunteers, Fabio Morani, Sergio Lana, and Guido Puletti were killed near Gornji Vakuf in Bosnia. They were bringing humanitarian aid. The letter sent by Sergio Lana's mother to her son's murderers confirms the great truth: where there is forgiveness, there is God:

"My name is Franca. I am Sergio Lana's mother. He and his friends Fabio and Guido were killed on the road from Gornji Vakuf to Novi Travnik, on Saturday, May 28, 1993. My son was only twenty years old and it was his fifth trip to Croatia and Bosnia. He was a volunteer carrying aid to your people. This time he was carrying food for Novi Travnik and Zavidovići. Sergio was a modest young man. He was good and willing to help anyone because for him, like me, there is no difference between Croatians, or Muslims, or Serbs. All he wanted to do was help those who suffer ... those in need.

Together we prayed for peace in your country. To those who killed my son ... my only son ... Please know how much his father and I loved him. Sergio has left so much emptiness in my heart ... But, I believe in God and know, for sure, that my Sergio and his friends are now with God in Heaven. I am writing this letter to tell you that I feel no bitterness towards those who killed him ... I forgive them. I was told that there was a woman in the group who did this ... I don't know if she is a mother but I hope the Lord will touch her heart ... hers and the hearts of those men with her ... so that they might understand that every man's life is sacred ... and should be respected. Only through our love for each other can peace reign in the world and in our hearts."

Pilgrims praying on Podbrdo Mountain

The White Army

In spite of the war, the pilgrims kept visiting Medjugorje. The French were the most numerous, followed by other Europeans. The mothers of Croatian soldiers also arrived. They went on foot in long procession, from Medjugorje to Križevac, praying to Our Lady for the protection of their sons. There were good people too, who transported refugees in vans and brought them to Medjugorje to pray and seek comfort from the Holy Mother because they had lost not only all their maternal belongings but many members of their families, too. Vicka took tender care of them.

The visionary Marija often talked with the members of the Spanish peacekeeping forces in Medjugorje. She told them about Our Lady's messages.

When the apparitions began Medjugorje was far away from the world ... now, it was the centre ... full of the United Nations' soldiers. Many of them discovered God there and became witnesses back in their own countries.

Often the UN "observers" dressed in white aboard in their white jeeps, could be seen driving along the roads. Here was the "white army" that old Marićiuša talked about fifty years earlier!

As the war was reaching its end, on the Feast of the Birth of the Virgin, 1993, the visionary Marija married the Italian Paolo Lunetti in Milan. Many were surprised by her decision and asked her if Our Lady had advised her so. She replied that She hadn't, because the Holy Mother does not interfere with anyone's free choice of action. Marija felt that by creating a family she would have more chance to transmit the Virgin's message than by retiring in a convent. There were many pilgrims in Italy who did not approve of her choice. Personally I believe that matrimony is also a very important holy vow. In the darkness which surrounds us we need these beacons of light. Moral and ethical values have fallen rapidly because women, whose duty it is to be a mother and teacher, have failed in their task.

By marriage Marija became a member of the Milanese diocese ... numerically the largest one in the world, because it is made-up of over five million parishioners. She continues to receive Our Lady's messages, not only for her small homeland parish, but for all the world too. This is why I believe she did the right thing by getting married and that she did not "end up" in Italy by chance.

Two months after Marija's wedding, Marijana Vasilj married Dinko Juričić from Čitluk. A few months later she lost the gift of interior locution. It did not surprise her because Our Lady had told both Jelena and her that they would not have this gift for life.

In October 1994 the visionary Ivan married Loreen Murphy, an American from Boston. Before meeting Ivan, Loreen won the beauty title of Miss Massachusetts and was launched on a promising career which she gave up to follow the Heavenly Mother's messages and to create a family with Ivan. It is not known if this wedding is a part of the secrets revealed to Ivan about his future life.

The most of visionaries, naturally gifted in learning foreign languages, which helps one remarkably to communicate with people from other countries, married people from abroad creating in this way a stronger bond beetwen Medjugorje and the rest of the world.

Our Lady appears to Marija during her marriage

Ivan's marriage, Father Slavko is present

The recent war interrupted the work of the committee established in order to investigate the authenticity of the apparitions. The last official statement is dated April 1991 and it leaves an open verdict still on the question of Medjugorje. However, it acknowledges, as from now, the necessity of pastoral and spiritual attention from the Church.

One can understand the cautious attitude of the Ecclesiastic Authorities: the young visionaries are still alive and some of them still (after a quoter of century) have daily apparitions.

One might ask why Pope John Paul II never went to Medjugorje himself, seeing that he travelled around the world so much. It seems that during a private audience, the Pope said to the visionary Mirjana:

"If I were not the Pope, I would already have been to Medjugorje."

As leader of the Church, the Pope must take into account certain canonical laws and proceedures which require prolonged and careful testing by various experts in the field. Cardinals, archbishops and bishops from all over the world have arrived in Medjugorje in answer to this high spiritual call ... but never in an official manner. However Medjugorje is widely recognized as a great Marian sanctuary.

Vicka prays and consoles a sick woman

Thanksgiving Pilgrimage

It was only in the Easter 1995 that I managed to return to Medjugorje. I was with my friends, the volunteers of the "Cuore Generoso" (Generous Heart), an organization from Ospedaletto Lodigiano. We wanted to thank Our Lady for everything we had managed to do, with Her help, for the people who had undergone the agony of the war. I returned brimming with spiritual energy which sustained me when, just two months later, my beloved daughter, aged only twenty-six, suddenly died of a natural death. It was a year and a half after the unexpected death of my mother.

Even though, as I mentioned earlier in this book, my daughter suffered from bad health from birth, when she died she was going through a good period health-wise ... in no way could we have foreseen her sudden death. My faith, which had been strengthened during my recent visit to Medjugorje helped me enormously ... preventing me from falling into the deepest desperation. The visionary Marija, who lives quite near me in Italy, came to comfort me. The prayers sustained me, giving me the energy and will to write the book "Dreaming of Lara". Through the book, I offered my experience to those who have also suffered the loss of a son or daughter, hoping that they, too, could find comfort through their faith.

As soon as I got over the shock, I went to Medjugorje with my father. In spite of being over eighty-five years of age he climbed both the Podbrdo and the Križevac hills with ease and here we prayed for our beloved deceased.

My father said that he wished a new house to be built on his land, in memory of Lara, with the aim of helping all children in difficulty. My husband and I immediately accepted the idea and we did our best to carry out his wishes. As if he had only been waiting for our agreement, a little while later my father passed away peacefully. After his wife and granddaughter he too had completed his mission on earth.

Soon after, while I was praying, I remembered his words of wisdom: "It is more important how you live, not how much money you have." I clearly remembered the last words of my mother: "God, help me!". I was moved to think of what my dearest daughter used to say in her moments of pain and suffering ... simply: "Amen, it will finish ...!"

From the left: Jakov, Ivan and Marija during the apparition; behind them Father Petar Ljubičić (1995)

259

By carrying out my father's wishes I now have the opportunity to go to Medjugorje quite often. My dearest relatives: grandparents, parents, uncles and aunts have all passed on to a better life. A new younger generation fills their houses with laughter and joy. My young relatives have replaced the old and they are pious and good, with the Queen of Peace to look after them and protect them.

Father Slavko with a great friend of the Croatian people,
Karl of Habsburg with his mother and his wife

What is the actual situation in the new Federation of Bosnia and Hercegovina which, by the Dayton Agreement of 1995, is in fact an international protectorate?

The Serbs are strong in Banja Luka, west of Bosnia, and have their own economic and political independence. Their enclave is almost ethnically "pure" because, of the two hunderd thousand Croatians that lived there before, only about three thousand returned. For the moment only Muslims have returned to the part of Bosnia governed by the Serbs. As for the capital city of Sarajevo, the Muslims are more numerous there, just as they are in other important cities in Bosnia too. Sadly, the Croats are in a clear minority throughout Bosnia and they still show a tendency ... to leave their country, probably forever, because from a practical point of view the impressive peace force does not seem to help them to return to the cities from which they were driven away during that cruel war. The Croats in Hercegovina form a compact nucleus which is however quite vulnerable. Their dream to be part of their mother country has faded. Now there is a distinct border between Croatia and Bosnia.

Cardinal Puljić of Sarajevo, Monsignor Franjo Komarica of Banja Luka and Monsignor Ratko Perić of Mostar, realizing the precarious and delicate position of the Croatian Catholics in the Bosnian Federation, sent petitions to the OHR (The Office of the High Representative) requesting full respect of the Croats' human rights... equal to those of the other two nations. The Bishops were criticised by the UN representatives because they interfere in political matters. Their reply to such accusations is simply that, if the Croats disappear from Bosnia, then there would not even be a Catholic Church which they, the bishops, represent.

Father Domej brings to Pope John Paul II as a gift the "Books" of Medjugorje" published by "Gebetsaktion" in Vienna

Despite the many difficulties, the stream of pilgrims to Medjugorje never ceases. Many arrive from the ex-Soviet Union, from the U.S.A., from Korea, the Philippines, Africa, Australia, Japan and the Lebanon. They are always surprised to see the helicopters of S-For, (the Stabilization Force), flying above the sanctuary ... usually during the celebration of the Holy Mass or while reciting the rosary. This often bothers them and distracts them from their prayers. Sometimes they also pass through the narrow roads in armed cars, obliging the pilgrims, who are perhaps descending the Apparitions Hill, to make way for them. Some time ago, the vicar in office, Father Ivan Sesar had asked the highest authorities of the S-For to be more respectful of the sanctuary.

Both during and after the war in their country, the visionaries became more and more ardent in spreading the word to various countries of the world.

On the 11th September 1998, the day before Jakov had his last daily meeting with Our Lady (and three years before the terrible terrorist attack in New York!), he was with visionary Mirjana and father Svetozar Kraljević in Florida on a mission. Suddenly during the aparition Holy Mother told Jakov that She would reveal the tenth secret to him next day.

When the vision ended Jakov remembered that Mirjana's daily visions had ceased after she received the 10th secret. He became afraid that the same thing would happen to him, even though, deep in his heart, he hoped they would continue. Bitter tears were shed as he asked himself how could he possibly survive without his visions?

The next day he was told the tenth secret and, while the Madonna spoke to him, She appeared very sad. Then She smiled and said:

"My dearest son, I am your Mother and I love you unconditionally. From today onwards, I shall no long appear to you every day but I will appear on Christmas Day, the day my Son was born. Do not be sad because I shall always be with you, as a mother and, like every true mother, I will never leave you. Continue to follow the way of my Son: the way of peace and love, and do your best to persevere in the mission that I have entrusted you with. Always be the example of a man who knows God and His love. Men will always see in you the example of how God works in, and through, men. I give you my maternal blessing and I thank you for answering my call."

When the vision finished, Jakov felt as if his heart had died, he wept bitterely to think that he had been brought up with the visions of the Holy Mother. Now, he asked himself, how would he survive without them? He felt alone, forsaken even though he was aware that the Holy Mother would always help him and that what really mattered was to feel her in his heart.

Marija visits Moscow

New Year's Eve 2000, saw as many pilgrims arriving in Medjugorje as in the summer season. We entered the Jubilee year dep in prayer: we exchanged wishes of peace and love. Around me were Japanese, Germans, Czechs, Ukrainians, Italians ... what a wonderful beginning to the millennium... giving hope for an even better tomorrow.

Vicka stood tirelessly on her balcony even during the summer of that Jubilee year, and thanks to an interpreter, her words reached the pilgrims who came from various countries of the former Soviet Union. Afterwards she received those pilgrims who needed particular advice or who wanted to entrust their prayers to her.

One day I too asked her advice: I was in doubt whether to up-date my old book about the apparitions written in Italian. When I sat down at my computer I started a new book in Italian then, half way through, I continued in Croatian ... my mother tongue! I explained to Vicka that I could not make out why I felt the urge to write about everything from the very beginning, before the apparitions. Vicka smiled at me and sweetly said: "Don't worry ... just write!" I went away from her in tears.

I continued to pray to the Madonna to help me express in my writings all that I felt in my heart as I went through so many years of apparitions. I whispered: "Thank you dear Mother because, by writing this book, You have offered me one more opportunity to convert."

Do not Neglect the Hills

During my full immersion in research about all the happenings at Medjugorje, I received the sad news of Father Slavko's unexpected death.

As usual, at about 2 o'clock on Friday, November 24, 2000, he had led the Way of the Cross up the Križevac Hill, as he had done for so many years. It was raining and, as the group started to walk down at about 15.30 after having finished the prayers and the blessing, the good Father warned them to be careful, while going down, not to slip and fall.

While they were all walking downhill, he suddenly collapsed on a rock then, looking up to the sky, he died. His heart failed him. His last words reveal his loving care for those who prayed with him and followed him. Those same words which, with his fine, Franciscan humour now take on another meaning: "Don't stop ... be careful not to slip down when I'm gone!"

When I heard he had passed away, I could not believe that Friar Slavko had left us forever ... just as so many other people who had met him, admired him and loved him could not believe it. Also Friar Slavko was only 54 years of age ... years well spent ... He wasted none of them!

I remembered what he recently had told on the Hill of Apparition, Podbrdo:

"I beg of you, do not neglect the Hills!"

Father Slavko celebrates the Eucharist on Križevac

His death offers many symbols: he died on a Friday afternoon after leading the Way of the Cross ... the same time as our Saviour Jesus Christ left His body. His death was a strong message for millions of pilgrims who, with Father Slavko's help, discovered their faith, or perhaps renewed it at Medjugorje.

During his lifetime, he received many hard blows from people near and far which made him suffer continually. While attempting to avoid those blows, he would limit himself to a small comment, he left the rest to time and to the Supreme Judge.

He was a priest, a true man of God, a missionary in the service of truth and the Holy Virgin. For twenty years, he wore himself out, preaching the messages of Our Lady and making them known to all the world. After so much hard work, the Lord called Father Slavko to Him when he was at his most spiritual condition.

He spoke five languages fluently and was known in every continent of the world. Only 15 minutes after his death, the whole world knew the sad news ... through internet. Millions of people mourned the departure of this extraordinary man ... the kind one meets only too rarely in a lifetime. One cannot say enough good things about him.

Friar Slavko incarnated love in action.

How is it possible to describe someone like him?

His mother, aged ninety-two, survived him. She had sent him to the seminary because they were so poor she could not even afford to buy him a pair of sandals. There he was given some sandals there, and there he stayed, long after them were worn out, because he realised that he was born to be a priest.

Father Slavko's mother

Father Slavko (1999)

When I saw Father Slavko for the last time one morning at the end of October 2000, after Mass, he was with a group of his protégés, ex-alcoholics and ex-homeless. He gave each of them a task and told me "You see them? They're good lads, they're discreet, reasonable, modest, they don't ask for anything and they make things easy for me!". Some of these 'good lads' carried the body of their benefactor down Mount Križevac to the parish house.

Some days before his death, Father Slavko had prayed with Vicka and he had confided in her that the bishop had ordered him to leave Medjugorje before Christmas. He told her that he, Slavko, would obey this order even though it was painful for him to have to leave.

Father Slavko and the visionary Vicka in 1984

Father Slavko died the day before the monthly message, which he had announced and commented for many years on Radio Maria. The seer, Marija, quickly arrived from Italy with her husband. She cried near his corpse as she awaited the apparition of Our Lady. As soon as the Holy Mother appeared, she asked Her why it had happened. Our Lady consoled her by saying that everything happens through God's Divine Will and She gave the following, comforting message:

"Dear children! Today when Heaven is especially near to you I call you to pray so that, trough your prayers, you put God first. Little children, today I am near you and I give each of you my motherly blessing so that you have the strength and love for all the people you meet in your earthly life and so you can give God's love. I rejoice with you and I wish to tell you that your brother Slavko has been born into Heaven and intercedes for you. Thank you for having responded to my call."

The new Chaplain, Father Ljubo Kurtović, was moved and commented this message on Radio Maria, in Italian, while substituting for Father Slavko for the first time.

On Sunday November, 26th, at 2 o'clock, a Requiem Mass was led by Bishop Perić. Some felt that his presence was a quiet acknowledgement that both he and his predecessor, Monsignor Žanić, had been too strict with Father Slavko when they insisted that he should be sent away from Medjugorje. They had not considered the extraordinary circumstances which requested his presence at this new sanctuary of Our Lady. I only hope with all my heart that, when the Bishop conducted the Requiem Mass, he felt the Blessed Virgin's presence and that he thanked Father Slavko for praying and fasting for him ... his Bishop.

Father Tomislav Pervan, the Provincial of the Franciscan order, said among other things: "Father Slavko lived three lives: he never rested; he got up before everyone else everyday and went to the Apparition Hill; he went to bed after everyone: a penitent hermit. He had taken his own personal cross to the Križevac ... the cross of Medjugorje ... the cross of the pilgrims and his Province."

The former Parish Priest, Father Ivan Landeka, who worked with Father Slavko for nine years, said, on taking his leave of him: "Everytime there was a decision to make, while we were still deciding, Father Slavko was already half way there! If he had a temperature, he would not go to bed ... he would just carry on working".

The German priest, Dietrich von Stockhausen, thanked Father Slavko because all the priests who attended his seminars on Our Lady's messages lived a spiritual rebirth.

On behalf of all the visionaries, Jakov thanked Father Slavko for having been their spiritual guide for so many years.

After an apparition (1984): Jakov, Vicka and Father Slavko

Many relatives, 122 priests, the visionaries, the parishioners and over ten thousand pilgrims from Bosnia and abroad attended his funeral. Flags were flown at half-mast for miles around and the shops closed for two days. Sadness filled the air.

The sound of the violin playing the touching melody, "Dear Mother We Have Come" was heard as Father Slavko's body was laid down in the tomb of Father Križan Galić, who was murdered by partisans during the Second World War ... a year before Father Slavko was born. Both of them died with a prayer on their lips. Both of them found their last resting place in the small cemetery of Medjugorje ... under the Križevac alongside those modest and devoted parishioners who, perhaps, has perpared the way for the apparitions with their prayers and fasting.

I think that, everytime I am in Medjugorje, I will hear Father Slavko's dear voice in my heart ... the voice I heard so often as he prayed. Thank you, Father Slavko, because you prayed even when I did not. I wish to take leave of you here by repeating your words regarding the parish of Medjugorje:

"The parish community of Medjugorje responded immediately right from the beginning of the apparitions. Now, however, there is the danger that they might forget their first experiences and their original promises and that they might lose sight of that love and initial fire. There is the real danger of spiritual oblivion in the parish and that relationships might become materialistic towards the Virgin Mary and towards others. It is a real danger but I am convinced that it will be overcome because there are people and entire families who follow the Virgin's messages in their lives and in their daily work.

There are also people, and this is a well known fact, who have lost all sense of religion and live thinking only of work, money and business. However, this should not surprise us because the Holy Mother, explained in one of Her messages that where She and Her Son appear, satan arrives and tries to destroy everything. Let us not forget that, without the parish community's participation, it would be difficult to imagine that the apparitions would have taken their course, as they did.

As for the effect the apparitions had on the daily lives of the parishioners ... I would suggest that the time in which the Virgin Mother appears should be a moment of holiness. It would be wonderful if all the shops, the restaurants and bars would stop working and recite the rosary during the Holy hour of the arrival of Our Heavenly Mother ... Everything would be so different!"

The Mothers' Village

Before leaving you, dear readers, I would like to linger a little on one of the fruits of the apparitions, the foundation of the "Mothers' Village" by Father Slavko.

Several years have passed but I still remember the meditations of Father Slavko on one of the central messages of the Holy Virgin: "The Lord can do nothing without you".

The Friar repeated the message slowly pronouncing each word, paused for a while and looked upon us with his kind, intellectual eyes and explained the words coming from his mystical mind:

"Our Lady doesn't want us to criticise or judge our fellow men, because we already know how to criticise and judge others. She is trying to teach us that we should be the first to love our neighbours and offer peace and reconciliation.

There is no one in the world who does not want to be loved, who doesn't want to live in peace. But, if no one loves, if no one brings peace, who can be loved, who can enjoy peace?"

Father Slavko paused again before he continued:

"If Our Lady wants the results to be seen, it's not for Herself...but for us. Those ready to reconcile themselves and work for their neighbour, already have the results. Who dares to start acting immediately without waiting for someone else to take the initiative? Jesus didn't wait, he didn't say: "I will wait for your conversion and then I will die for you". Had He done that, He would still not be dead! Instead, without imposing any kind of condition, He sacrificed Himself on the cross for you and for me."

Father Slavko in action: leading the Way of the Cross on Križevac; reciting the Rosary on Podbrdo Hill and giving blessings in the church

Never tiring, Father Slavko lived the messages from day to day. Through his work, he showed the connecting lines that form a perfect triangle, the three cardinal points chosen by Our Lady: the Hill of the apparitions, the Mountain of the Cross and the church of Saint James:

- Ascending Podbrdo hill, he recited the Rosary and prepared the faithful for the intimate, personal meeting with the "Queen of Peace".

- Leading the Way of the Cross on Mount Križevac, devoting himself and his followers to Christ, the Redeemer.

- Praying in the church every evening on his knees and reminding the faithful during Holy Mass of the importance Our Lady gives in Her messages to prayer and the Sacraments of Reconciliation and the Eucharist.

The three cardinal pints of Medjugorje: Podbrdo, Križevac and St. James church. On the left, the statue of Fr. Slavko

During the night, while the village slept, he would write at his desk, producing many books inspired by the Marian messages:

"Pray With the Heart"; "Give Me Your Wounded Heart"; "Celebrate Mass with the Heart"; "In the School of Love"; "Adore My Son With the Heart"; "Pray Together with a Joyful Heart"; "Fast with the Heart"; "Pearls of the Wounded Heart"; "The Way of the Cross" and various interviews. (The books have been translated into more than twenty languages and can be purchased in the parish book shop in Medjugorje.)

Many years before the apparitions started, Father Slavko was well known for being extremely helpful to his neighbours. It is worth remembering that, as a young chaplain, he even helped the students to overcome their problems with mathematics, German and other subjects. When a child had a problem, the mother would say, "Go to Father Slavko, he will help you!" And he would help not once, but hundreds of times.

Having been brought up in the Marian school, his service to the needy became more ardent over the years. He would affectionately work harder with those who had fallen from the straight path. He was convinced that it was never too late to help those who had fallen victim to vice, since each person has a precise duty on earth and quite often a hidden talent to discover.

Therefore, he believed that no one should ever be abandoned, even if his soul is almost destroyed and his body drugged. In him, the 'good boys' and those from the community "Cenacolo" in Medjugorje had an affectionate father who will be difficult to substitute.

At the outbreak of the recent Balkan war, Father Slavko started to look ahead. He founded the "Mothers' Village" for orphans and neglected children, pregnant and abandoned women, a nursery school and a health center for retarded children.

One day, Father Slavko went into the overgrown wooded area on the outskirts of Medjugorje with some of his assistants and Schwanhild Heintschel-Heinegg, who also helped him maintain contacts with benefactors from around the world. As they were making their way through the thicket, Father Slavko told his friends: "I have a dream! I would like to make a park out of this rubbish dump: here we could have lakes, some animals for the children to play with, a playground for the children and a place for meditation for the elderly, who cannot climb the hills!"

While his thoughts were pouring out of him, his robe kept getting caught by of the bushes. His friends followed him in disbelief, trying to keep up with him and thinking that now he was really dreaming - that this could not be done. But for Father Slavko nothing was impossible!

Father Slavko went to the Council and had the land donated to him. He called all his "good kids" and, together, they burned the rubbish and cleared the land. Within a short period of time, Father Slavko's dream has become a reality for everyone to see and enjoy.

In Father Slavko's vision there was no ghetto for orphans, retarded or mutilated children...No! He wanted a home that would take in the children of the families of Medjugorje, together with his orphans, abandoned children, the disabled, the retarded, so that they could grow up together and that they would have the opportunity to help each other right from early childhood.

Being the good psychologist that he was, Father Slavko said that the psychological traumas of children who live through the cruelties of "warfare" within their own families, are often more serious than those due to actual war.

This brings to my mind the big, frightened and lost "Bambi" eyes of a boy from the north of Bosnia, now at Mothers' Village. Born of a mixed Catholic and Muslim family, he was torn between his parents who had drug problems. He came to the village longing for love, and finally found it there in a new family, with the result that his "Bambi" eyes shone again.

Fr. Slavko on the merry-go-round
with a boy from the 'Mothers' village'

Just six months after the death of Father Slavko, a statue depicting him giving a blessing with the cross in his hand was erected in the centre of the village. It was made by an old friend of his, the Italian artist Carmelo Puzzolo, the same artist who made the statue of the Croatian saint Leopold Mandić (in the church square) and whom Father Slavko had entrusted with the creation of the stations of the Cross on Križevac and those of the Rosary on Apparitions Hill.

Two recitals at 'Mother's village' in the presence of Fr. Slavko

More than once, I have stopped near the statue of Father Slavko and while praying, have felt his presence, even though there is an atmosphere of eternity wich makes him unreachable. Strangely it seems that he is encouraging me to do what I can to continue where he left of. For this reason, I have decided that the profits from this book will go to the Mothers' Village.

In these previous pages, I have written about the first period of over two decades of apparitions, wich coincides with the time during which Father Slavko offered his utmost assistance to the visionaries and the pilgrims.

With his undisputed charisma and his knowledge of languages, he did all he could to ensure that the message of peace and conversion of the "Queen of Peace" is spread around the world efficiently and clearly.

Only the future will show us just how faithful Father Slavko was to the ideals of the founder of his religious order, Saint Francis, and how much he loved God and his neighbour.

A week before his death, with an enigmatic smile, Father Slavko said in an interview with a Film troupe from Munich:

"I should have complexes: I am in contact with those who say that they see Our Lady, while I see nothing! I am in contact with those who say that they feel with the heart, while I feel nothing! What's more, I often meet those who photograph everything, even that which I can't see..!"

Fr. Slavko in typical poses in his belowed wood at the M. Village

Fr. Slavko plays with the childern in the 'Mothers village'

These words make us realise that he was not searching for the sensational side of the apparitions... that he did not want to become a protagonist, but that he was convinced that the message from the Virgin Mary should be lived with our whole being.

During his last homily, the morning of his death, Father Slavko said to a group of Austrians led by Mr. Franz Gollowitsch, who was on his 250th pilgrimage to Medjugorje "Our Lady finishes every message with the words: 'Thank you for having responded to my call'. I have often asked myself whom Mary comes to thank so much, to come from Heaven and say thank you. She doesn't expect too much from us, She sees all the good we do and thanks us for that. I too would like to say thank you, with Mary, to all these people, who have responded to Her messages in their own ways. We need to hear what She often says.. that..., without us, She can do nothing."

Father Slavko lived the maternal message; he prayed and fasted tirelessly and devotedly for many long years.

A true martyr of conscience, he offered all of himself and his own suffering to Christ, in accordance with his faith, until he breathed his last breath on Križevac, still praying and blessing those who followed him.

This is the spiritual legacy he has left us.

Thank you Father Slavko, God be with you!

With Christ in the Third Millennium

In the early morning of the 25th of June 2001, the twentieth anniversary of the beginning of the apparitions, the parishioner Iva Šego left home for the church as usual reciting the Rosary and passed by the small local cemetery where Father Slavko rests in the bosom of the Lord. She picked up the consumed candles and arranged the flowers before praying at his tomb.

The day was clear and already hot in the early morning, just as it had been two decades before, in 1981.

The car park near the cemetery was filling up with the cars of pilgrims who were welcomed to Medjugorje by large posters proclaiming: "With Christ into the Third Millennium!"

Some of them came immediately to the tomb of the dear Friar who many times before had welcomed them to Medjugorje with open arms and an unforgettable smile.

Suddenly, finding herself surrounded by people from all over the world, Iva got up and tiptoed out of the cemetery; she went to the church square where many parishioners were waiting for the morning Mass.

They were talking amongst themselves about the grand jubilee of the twentieth anniversary of the apparitions and the great crowd of pilgrims that had already arrived in Medjugorje, and also about the other extraordinary jubilee: that day wa to be celebration of 50th and 60th anniversaries of when the Medjugorje brothers, Vinko and Marko Dragičević entered the priesthood.

The brothers, Fathers Vinko and Marko

Fr. Slavko Soldo shows the gifts from the Pope to the Friars Vinko and Marko

Zealous Iva was also present at the solemn Mass at eleven in a church full of people. At the altar, next to the two brothers, there was also their sister, a Franciscan nun, and two nephews, also Franciscan monks. Behind them were Father Dobroslav Stojić and Father Leonard Oreč who had been for many years in the service of Medjugorje and had recently celebrated their fiftieth anniversaries too.

During the solemn celebration, the new Provincial, Father Slavko Soldo, also a native of Medjugorje, showed the assembly the parchment with the congratulations from the Pope for the Dragičević brothers.

The prayers of the faithful also remembered Father Stanko Vasilj (you may remember the author of the hymn: "We come to you Dear Mother") and Father Slavko Barbarić, an adopted son of Medjugorje who had passed away there and was immediately welcomed into Heaven.

This great day of grace, so full of significance, gave the people of Medjugorje a chance to reflect on the true values that should be preserved, even in a new consumer-type life-style. One hopes that these people and future generations will not forgot the vows of faith their predecessors made to Jesus Christ, the Catholic Church (universal and apostolic) and the eternal values of a Christian, and that they will always be led by priests like Father Slavko, of high moral standing and totally consecrated to Our Lady: "Totus tuus", following the edifying example of Pope John Paul II.

The same hope goes for the visionaries who are now all married. The last wedding August 2002 was that of Jelena to Massimiliano Valente from Rome. Before them in January 2001, Vicka married Mario Mijatović who was a close colla-borator of Father Slavko in the "Mother's Village".

The marriages of Vicka and of Jelena

The families and relatives of the visionaries now lead dignified lives, even though they never have a moment's peace because of the long procession of curious pilgrims knocking on their doors. A few pilgrims show surprise at the fact that the visionaries have not stayed "as poor as church mice". To those who have spoken to me about this I always reply: "If providence has brought a certain well-being to this poor parish, where is it written that the visionaries, who lead lives of great sacrifice, should go hungry or without a roof over their head? Jesus Himself tells us in the Gospel that if our Heavenly Father takes care of the birds in the sky, so much more will he take care of those who serve Him".

Marija with her son   *Jakov with his daughter*

The families of the visionaries are still growing.

Mirjana lives in the hamlet of Bijakovići and has two daughters: Marija and Veronika. She continues to serve the pilgrims to the best of her ability and on the second day of every month the Holy Mother prays with her for those who deny God's existence, in the presence of hundreds of pilgrims from all parts of the world.

Jakov, timid as usual, lives near the visionary Mirjana and has three childern: Arianna Maria, David Emanuel and Miriam Chiara. Sometimes he gives his testimony to the pilgrims.

Marija lives between Medjugorje and Monza, Italy. She is the mother of four boys: Michele Maria, Francesco Maria, Marco Maria and Giovanni Maria. After three sons she had hoped for a girl, but the Lord gave her the gift of another son and Marija said: "That's all right...maybe when he grows up, he will become a missionary". Marija passes on her monthly message to the whole world.

Marijana lives at Čitluk with her husband, mother-in-law and three daughters: Anamarija, Olga and Franka. Always calm and serene, she occasionally gives her testimony to the groups of pilgrims.

Ivan lives between Medjugorje and the United States. He travels a great deal, talking about his experience. He never tires of saying that the young are in danger because their parents are taken up with material worries and don't spend as much time as they should on their up-bringing. Ivan has two doughters: Cristina and Michela and a son Daniel.

Jelena lives in Rome. After having studied philosophy in the USA and theology in Vienna, she got her degree in the History of the Church at the Gregorian University of Rome, and a second degree in ancient Hebrew at the University for Bible Studies in Rome. She has two sons: Giovanni Paolo and Agostino. Jelena asserts that every moment in life is an opportunity to be an apostle and that, through the Sacrament of marriage, her personal relationship with God has become deeper.

286

Vicka, the radiant mother of a daughter, Sofija Marija, and a son, Ante, lives at Krehin Gradac, near Medjugorje and continues to unselfishly testify from the balcony of her old family house at Bijakovići.

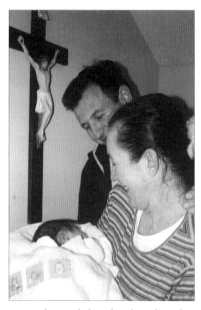

Vicka with her husband and daughter

Vicka receive the pilgrims just after becoming a mother

Those who, like me, know the visionaries personally, know that they are simple and sincere, both when they transmit the messages and when they speak of their daily lives. Each one of them has a precise duty in prayer: for the souls in Purgatory, for the priesthood, for the families, and for those who do not know God... As I have already said, Marija hopes that at least one of her children will become a missionary; Vicka speaks of the joy that her childern gives her; Jelena confides that she feels closer to God since she has entered the sacrament of marriage.

Mirjana, Ivanka and Jakov do not hide the fact that they must work harder than the others on the road to holiness because the eyes of the world are still upon them, although the daily apparitions have ceased.

The simple testimonies of the visionaries are not banalities but indications of the path to follow, for those who want to understand. The daily apparitions experienced by Marija, Vicka and Ivan could stop tomorrow, or continue for as long as they live. This is no longer important. The message of Our Lady has been transmitted around the world through them. Just think...the message of the Holy Virgin has even reached a tribe in Australia which, until fifty years ago, still practiced cannibalism...

Two joung pilgrims and Iva Šego,
who spends several hours every
day in prayer

288

What about the people of Medjugorje? Where do they stand after so many years of apparitions? Some have made a good business selling gasoline or trading wholesale souvenirs. Others are badly-paid civil servants, while the majority make their living catering for the pilgrims. Most of the hotels and souvenir stores are managed by foreigners. Those families who, right from the beginning of the apparitions, put up the pilgrims free of charge and paid the fines for doing so, now live a life of hardship and poverty. They have few rooms and they rarely put up the pilgrims, who usually arrive in groups and prefer the hotels to their simple accommodation. Yet they are the ones who attend Mass regularly ... they are the ones who pray and fast for the Queen of Peace's purpose.

Even though there are obscure forces doing their best to deny or corrupt the Marian message of peace and reconciliation, a watchful eye will note that, in Medjugorje, there is a presence of Protestant, Anglican and Orthodox priests who come to pray alongside the Catholics for the unity of the Church. People follow this example as, in their hearts, they wish to see the Church of Christ become a unified church. The signs of the times, which are changing for the better, are recognizable wherever the words of the "Queen of Peace" have arrived, but it is not my job to talk of this more than I already have done.

The time will come when the protagonists, whom you may have met personally or through the pages of this book, will no longer be with us.

Our Lady knows that none of us have enough time at our disposal, that's why Her message is essential:

"Dear children, this is a time of grace! Pray to feel God in your hearts, and the rest will follow!"

We go back to the 15th of April 1984, Palm Sunday, when two young people from Medjugorje, Slavica Vasilj and Vinko Dragičević (nephew of the celebrating fathers, pag. 283) took a gift to the Pope John Paul II: a wooden cross with the messages from Our Lady at Medjugorje inscribed on it. On the pedestal there was a small statue of Our Lady and the date 25.06.1981. On the vertical pole at the top there was written: Mir (peace), at the bottom Obraćenje (conversion), on the horizontal arm to the left the word Molitva (prayer) and to the right Post (fasting). In the centre only the year 1981. The Pope touched the cross, carefully read the messages in Croatian and finally said: "These messages are evangelical." The Pope then said farewell to the two Croatians and gave them his apostolic blessing.

Throughout his Papacy, this great Marian Pope continuously called for prayer and conversion, and for believers to live daily by the Gospel. "Do not be afraid, open the doors to Christ! Convert!" These words are still felt in the hearts of millions of believers, bravely reminded by the Holy Father to give up the widespread and fearful practice of abortion and other deviations that are not worthy of the children of God.

The last image of the Pope at his window, silent, closer to his Lord through his suffering, touched the world. He could not speak, so he used his hand and eyes to greet us. Seeing his suffering, I felt in my heart the words he would have said: "I have guided you as far as I can, I love you and I leave you in the hands of Her to whom I have dedicated all my existence. Totus tuus!"

At 21.37 on the 2nd of April 2005 Pope Wojtyla left us.

At the same time in the U.S.A it was still daytime. The visionary Ivan was at the great prayer meeting being held in the Church of St. Patrick and Joakim in New Hampshire. After the recital of the Rosary he had his daily vision.

The e-mail Ivan wrote to his family and friends in Medjugorje said:

"Dear ones, here we are all saddened by the death of the Holy Father and I know that you are too. We are all nothing but pilgrims on this earth. We are passing through. Now I will describe the vision of the 2nd of April 2005. That late Saturday afternoon I went to bear witness in the Church of St. Patrick and Joakim in New Hampshire, we all recited the rosary together and at about 18.40 h Our Lady appeared to me radiant with joy and She greeted us: "The Lord be praised my children!" After the greeting the (Gospa) held Her hands over the whole assembly and blessed us with Her maternal blessing. I recommended all those present to Her, especially the sick.

All of a sudden, the image of the Holy Father appeared to Her left. He was smiling. Our Lady turned gently towards him and looked at him with immense joy, saying to me "Dear son, here is my son, he is with me". As suddenly as it had appeared the image of the Holy Father disappeared and I continued to speak to Our Lady. The apparition lasted eight minutes. Whilst I write to you I am still excited by the event and I cannot find the words to express my emotion and joy."

In the Holy Year 2000, Pope John Paul II entrusted the new Millennium to Our Lady, proclaimed the Year of the Rosary, adding the new mysteries of the Light to the prayers of the devotees of the Most Holy Virgin. The Pope died in the Year of the Eucharist, the centre of Christian life.

His successor Pope Benedict XVI has taken his name from the patron of Europe, the old Christian continent which is becoming more lay and denying its roots. It is up to us to help the new Pope with our prayers, not to be afraid to suffer for our faith and to inscribe in our hearts the words of the new Shepherd of the Church: "The world cannot be saved by the crucifiers but only by the Crucified!"

We pay our respects to the dear great Pope John Paul II, remembering his words: "Open the doors to Christ" which the new Pope has already adopted, and which we too would be wise to adopt.

In Medjugorje, People are Turning to God

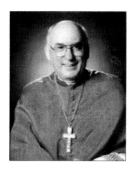

Arcbishop
Harry J. Flynn

Some years ago when I was first a bishop in Louisiana, it must have been 1988, I was making my first "ad limina" visit to the Holy Father in Rome. The other bishops of Louisiana were with me and, as what the custom of John Paul II, we were invited in to enjoy a lunch with him. There were eight of us at the table with him. Soup was being served. Bishop Stanley Ott of Baton Rouge, Louisiana, who has since gone to God, asked the Holy Father: "Holy Father, what do you think of Medjugorje?"

The Holy Father kept eating his soup and responded: "Medjugorje? Medjugorje? Medjugorje? Only good things are happening at Medjugorje. People are praying there. People are going to Confession. People are adoring the Eucharist, and people are turning to God. And, only good things seem to be happening at Medjugorje."

That seemed to have ended the discussion and we went on to another topic. But, I will long remember the very skillfully cautious response of our Holy Father.

Just two weeks ago, I had an opportunity to visit Medjugorje. A good friend for more than 50 years, Jim McHale from Connecticut, has been wanting to go to Medjugorje for some time. His wife was not inclined to go at this time for many reasons but mostly because she is preparing for the marriage of their daughter in New York City.

We flew from Minneapolis to Amsterdam, from Amsterdam to Prague and from Prague to Split in Croatia. We remained in Croatia for two evenings before we traveled up the mountain to Medjugorje in Bosnia along the Adriatic Sea. It is quite an adventure in arriving in this little mountain village which has apparently become famous because of the alleged apparitions that take place there. We were fortunate enough to have made contact with Stephanie Percic from Minneapolis. Stephanie was making her 100th pilgrimage to Medjugorje and leading a group of people from the Twin Cities, Crookston and Duluth and some from other parts of the country. Having been there so many times, Stephanie is well-known to the villagers. Certainly that helped us a great deal in getting about.

The drive from Split into Medjugorje is a beautiful one, indeed. The road snakes around the Adriatic Sea and up the mountain. At times it might seem a bit perilous but the beauty if overwhelmingly inviting. We arrived in the village on a Friday afternoon. There were 30,000 to 40,000 pilgrims there for the weekend. I was quite impressed with them all. They were from all over the world; countries throughout Europe, the United States, Ireland, Canada and the Philippines. Italy was well represented also.

On Saturday morning we heard one of the visionaries speak and I must say that everything that he said was very solid. Someone in the audience asked him a question about "Communion in the hand." His answer was very direct and very simple. "Do what the Church permits you to do. You will always be safe."

The great moment, for me, was the hearing of confessions every afternoon from 5 p.m. until 10 or 10:30 p.m. There were 46 priests hearing confessions in various languages. What a great grace that is onto itself: "People turning toward God."

I just walked around and looked at the lines. There were 26 confessional stations in which there was a priest and then 20 more priests hearing confessions in temporary stations. This happened also on Sunday afternoon from 5 p.m. until about 8:30 p.m. I heard confessions in English, and it was a great grace for me and a wonderful experience.

The Chapel of Adoration was most edifying. People came in quietly to adore the Eucharistic Lord and to pray.

Everything seemed to have been so orderly and quiet, as were the groups of people in the streets and on the hills saying their Rosary and praying.

I celebrated the noon Mass on Sunday in English. The church was packed to overflowing. There are pews outside on all three sides of the church in which people can hear the Mass but they cannot see it. Once again the faith of so many people touched me deeply.

This past week we celebrated the feast of St. Ignatius of Antioch. In his letter to the Romans, Ignatius wrote: "Within me is the living water which says deep inside me: 'Come to the Father.' "There is something of that yearning in all of those pilgrims who visited Medjugorje. Somehow there is something deep within them which keeps crying out, "Come to the Father. "They do this through devotion. They do it through their love for Mary. They do it through their love for Jesus Christ. "Come to the Father" is deep within each of one us.

On Monday morning, our pilgrimage was coming to a close. I celebrated Mass in the chapel of the Eucharist for the pilgrims who were led by Stephanie Percic. So many of them were from the Archdiocese of St. Paul and Minneapolis, and I was impressed by their strong faith and their promise of prayer for the entire archdiocese.

All in all, after the journey to Medjugorje, I keep pondering the words of John Paul II as he was eating his soup on that day sometime in 1988: "Medjugorje? Medjugorje? Medjugorje? Only good things seem to be happening at Medjugorje. People are turning to God."

(Published in the St. Paul-Minneapolis archdiocesan newspaper, The Catholic Spirit, October 19, 2006 and in http://www.spirit-daily.org)

Cardinal Schönborn from Vienna celebrates Holy Mass in Medjugorje, New Year 2010

Cardinal Schönborn's catechesis in the parish of Medjugorje

During his homily at the New Year's Eve Mass, Cardinal Schönborn said the following:

"Dear brothers and sisters here in the church and on the squares in front of the church and in the yellow hall. We are all conscious of the fact that it is a big privilege to not have to celebrate the New Year with champagne."

The crowd laughed, and the Cardinal added *"Maybe later"*, which was followed by laughter and clapping.

He continued: *"But now we are allowed to celebrate the beginning of the New Year with Mary and Joseph and with the Child that is lying in the manger and with the shepherds. These days, we have all come to Medjugorje to be especially close to the Mother of the Lord. To be more exact, we have to say that we have come here because we know that the Mother of the Lord wants to be close to us.*

With Her, we want to begin the New Year. And the first thing that moves me, when I think about the manger and the shepherds, is that there were no angels present. Although here there is an angel at the nativity set, but in the Gospel there are no angels waiting there. They were on the field with the shepherds... an entire host of angels. But Mary and Joseph only heard about it. The shepherds told them.

You also didn't see the Gospa. But there are people here who told about it. And we trust that the Mother of God really is close to us. Belief comes from hearing. And it impresses me that first, in the Gospel of today, there is talk about hearing. We have to listen to the good news first. We have two ears, two eyes, and only one mouth. That means we have to listen much, watch much, and then talk also. And what are we supposed to say? We are supposed to report what we have seen and heard. The world needs a new evangelization and that is only possible through people for whom it is impossible to keep silent about what they have seen and heard.

We all have received the faith. And through baptism we all have received the task to pass on the faith. The shepherds related what they were told. And from there it went on. The Gospel, the good news was told and those who told it were believable. Those who heard also saw that the word and life harmonize, that what the witnesses saw is also true in their life.

How can we be witnesses of the good news? First, by looking to Mary. Mary kept all that happened in Her heart and pondered it. Brothers and sisters, what we need most in this time is prayer. I'm saying this with a sadness of some sorts. I know that I'm praying not enough. I know that prayer is life. Without the living relationship with God our life becomes dry end empty.

What does the Mother of God tell us all the time? Pray. Take yourself time for prayer. Is that a good resolution for the New Year? For us priests and deacons. For us all. Time for prayer. It gives so much strength and so much joy. So much clarity. Let us ask Mary that She helps us to pray more. When we pray our word is also filled with life. And then our testimony is credible.

I want to tell you something about what the Apostle Paul told us. The Year of Paul is already over, we are now in the Year of Priests. But the word of the Apostle Paul was so strong because it was filled with life. In the Reading of today he talks about God sending His Son so that we can become sons. The daughters are not excluded here. Daughters and sons are meant together. But Paul says we are called to become sons, not slaves. Like Jesus is Son of God we are supposed to be allowed to call God Father. In the beginning of this year the Apostle Paul tells us: "You are sons and not slaves".

I believe Medjugorje is a place where a lot of people confess. Confession is deliverance from the slavery of sin. Nothing makes us less free than sin. God wants us as sons: Freedom of the children of God. And for that He gifted us with the sacrament of reconciliation. We are to have a new relationship with God, to be allowed to call Him Abba. Jesus invited us to that in a way that we trust Him, that we trust God. There is so much fear of God in us (or, "we are so afraid of God")."

The cardinal went on to say *"Jesus, I trust in you,"* in Croatian and Polish, and then continued: *"Pope John Paul II left us this message: "Trust in the mercy of God. Trust in the mercy of Jesus".*

Trust can be heroic sometimes, if life becomes difficult. If a marriage becomes a burden, if an illness oppresses us, if we don't know what becomes of our work; then to say Jesus I Trust in You; that can be heroic. Trust; that really is an act of faith. And again we look to Mary. Who has made and gave this act of trust, of faith, more than Mary? Jesus I Trust in You. That is to be our program in the coming year."

It is almost midnight and it is cracking, the cardinal said as he pointed towards the firecrackers going off outside. *"But we are not cracking, we are praying. We are not cracking but we are singing.*

And a last word: The shepherd returned, praised God, praised Him for what they heard and saw. We, too, will return home. In order that we can become witnesses of the Gospel, we have to praise God first. The shepherds praised God for what they have seen and heard. I hope that we can all drive home, travel home after these days here and praise God for what we have seen and heard. Then people will also believe us when we tell, then our word will be credible.

Now it is almost midnight. It is exactly the right moment to profess our faith. With this faith we are going into the New Year. God bless this year."

Cardinal Schönborn and the visionary Marija Pavlović on Apparition Hill

Index

Medjugorje: a Gift for the World

This Book is Available in the "Mother´s Village"
Bijakovići - Medjugorje

Tel.: 00387 36 653 001, e-mail: vita@tel.net.ba, www.mothersvillage.org

*Children of the Mother´s Village with their teachers
and the author of this book (second on the right)*

The "Mother´s Village" is financed exclusively through donations!

Donation account:
Bank ref.: UniCredit Bank d.d.
SWIFT: UNCRBA 22, IBAN BA 393380604802781703
Account: 5020120/48-06-027817

Readers say:

"Dear Mirjana, my congratulations for the success of your book and I am glad because of your apostolic work. I wish the book Our Lady's call from Medjugorje will be diffused throughout the whole world and do lots of good. I bless you in Christ and Mary."

(Father Gabriele Amorth, Rome)

"The book Our Lady's call from Medjugorje is phenomenal. I think this was Our Lady's call to you."

(Father Miljenko Šteko, BiH)

"The book is a strong evidence of the Virgin Mary's love for each one of us."
(Wolfgang, Germany)

"Many readers will be touched by this book."

(Father Nikolaj, Moscow)

This Book is also available in Medjugorje:

- in the Parish Bookshop
- in **Promocija**

You can find this book in BREILLE by:

RNIB Transcription Centre South West –
RNIB Registered Charity Number: 226227
Website: http://www.rnib.org.uk
Contact: shop@rnib.org.uk

Near Promocija you can visit **St. Charbel's Center: Mother of Life** and pray for unborn children and get the fliers to advertise the Vigil for life in your parishes.